Facebook

3rd Edition

the missing manual®

The book that should have come with the site

E.A. Vander Veer

O'REILLY®

Beijing | Cambridge | Farnham | Köln | Sebastopol | Tokyo

Facebook: The Missing Manual, Third Edition

BY E.A. VANDER VEER

Published by O'Reilly Media, Inc., 1005 Gravenstein Highway North, Sebastopol, CA 95472.

O'Reilly books may be purchased for educational, business, or sales promotional use. Online editions are also available for most titles (*http://my.safaribooksonline.com*). For more information, contact our corporate/institutional sales department: 800.998.9938 or *corporate@oreilly.com*.

Editor: Dawn Mann

Production Editor: Nellie McKesson

Compositor: Dessin Designs

Indexer: Lucie Haskins

Cover Designer: Karen Montgomery

Interior Designer: Ron Bilodeau

Print History:

January 2008:	First Edition.
April 2010:	Second Edition.
February 2011:	Third Edition.

ISBN: 9781449397418

[M]

Contents

The Missing Credits

About the Author

E.A. Vander Veer started out in the software trenches, lexing and yaccing and writing shell scripts with the best of them. She remained busy and happy for years writing C++ programs and wresting data from recalcitrant databases. After a stint as an Object Technology Evangelist (yes, that's an actual job title), she found a way to unite all her passions: writing about cool computer stuff in prose any human being can understand. Books followed—over a dozen so far—including *PowerPoint 2007: The Missing Manual*, *JavaScript for Dummies*, *XML Blueprints*, and the fine tome you're holding right now. She lives in Texas with her husband and daughter. Email: *eamoore@gmail.com*.

About the Creative Team

Dawn Mann (editor) is Associate Editor for the Missing Manual series. When not working, she beads, plays soccer, and causes trouble. Email: *dawn@oreilly.com*.

Nellie McKesson (production editor) spends most of her spare time doing DIY home renovation projects and dabbling in the arts.

Daniel Murphey (technical reviewer) is an aspiring author and avid reader who never truly grew up.

Lucie Haskins (indexer) lives in Woodland Park, Colorado. She became an indexer in 2000, after a long career in corporate America, with roles that ranged from computer programmer to management consultant. She specializes in embedded indexing for books on computer- and business-related topics. She loves to share her passion for indexing by talking about it to whoever will listen! Visit her site at luciehaskins.com for more information about indexing.

Acknowledgements

Muchisimas gracias to the Missing Manual editorial team—y'all truly are second to none. Special thanks go to Peter Meyers for originally suggesting this book, and for overseeing the entire process with wisdom and grace. Dawn Mann's top-notch editing buffed the manuscript to a high sheen, and tech reviewer Daniel Murphey triple-checked it for accuracy and currency (no mean feat when you're writing about a website so popular it spits out new features faster than Hollywood spits out buddy movies). A smart, nimble team like this one is every writer's dream.

The Missing Manual Series

Missing Manuals are witty, superbly written guides to computer products that don't come with printed manuals (which is just about all of them). Each book features a handcrafted index; cross-references to specific pages (not just chapters); and RepKover, a detached-spine binding that lets the book lie perfectly flat without the assistance of weights or cinder blocks.

Recent and upcoming titles include:

Access 2007: The Missing Manual by Matthew MacDonald

Access 2010: The Missing Manual by Matthew MacDonald

Buying a Home: The Missing Manual by Nancy Conner

CSS: The Missing Manual, Second Edition, by David Sawyer McFarland

Creating a Web Site: The Missing Manual, Second Edition, by Matthew MacDonald

David Pogue's Digital Photography: The Missing Manual by David Pogue

Droid X: The Missing Manual by Preston Gralla

Dreamweaver CS4: The Missing Manual by David Sawyer McFarland

Dreamweaver CS5: The Missing Manual by David Sawyer McFarland

Excel 2007: The Missing Manual by Matthew MacDonald

Excel 2010: The Missing Manual by Matthew MacDonald

FileMaker Pro 10: The Missing Manual by Susan Prosser and Geoff Coffey

FileMaker Pro 11: The Missing Manual by Susan Prosser and Stuart Gripman

Flash CS4: The Missing Manual by Chris Grover with E.A. Vander Veer

Flash CS5: The Missing Manual by Chris Grover

Google Apps: The Missing Manual by Nancy Conner

The Internet: The Missing Manual by David Pogue and J.D. Biersdorfer

iMovie '08 & iDVD: The Missing Manual by David Pogue

iMovie '09 & iDVD: The Missing Manual by David Pogue and Aaron Miller

iMovie '11 & iDVD: The Missing Manual by David Pogue and Aaron Miller

iPad: The Missing Manual by J.D. Biersdorfer

iPhone: The Missing Manual, Fourth Edition, by David Pogue

iPhone App Development: The Missing Manual by Craig Hockenberry

iPhoto '08: The Missing Manual by David Pogue

iPhoto '09: The Missing Manual by David Pogue and J.D. Biersdorfer

iPhoto '11: The Missing Manual by David Pogue and Lesa Snider

iPod: The Missing Manual, Eighth Edition, by J.D. Biersdorfer and David Pogue

JavaScript: The Missing Manual by David Sawyer McFarland

Living Green: The Missing Manual by Nancy Conner

Mac OS X: The Missing Manual, Leopard Edition by David Pogue

Mac OS X Snow Leopard: The Missing Manual by David Pogue

Microsoft Project 2007: The Missing Manual by Bonnie Biafore

Microsoft Project 2010: The Missing Manual by Bonnie Biafore

Netbooks: The Missing Manual by J.D. Biersdorfer

Office 2007: The Missing Manual by Chris Grover, Matthew MacDonald, and E.A. Vander Veer

Office 2010: The Missing Manual by Nancy Connor, Chris Grover, and Matthew MacDonald

Office 2008 for Macintosh: The Missing Manual by Jim Elferdink

Office 2010 for Macintosh: The Missing Manual by Chris Grover

Palm Pre: The Missing Manual by Ed Baig

PCs: The Missing Manual by Andy Rathbone

Personal Investing: The Missing Manual by Bonnie Biafore

Photoshop CS4: The Missing Manual by Lesa Snider

Photoshop CS5: The Missing Manual by Lesa Snider

Photoshop Elements 7: The Missing Manual by Barbara Brundage

Photoshop Elements 8 for Mac: The Missing Manual by Barbara Brundage

Photoshop Elements 8 for Windows: The Missing Manual by Barbara Brundage

Photoshop Elements 9: The Missing Manual by Barbara Brundage

PowerPoint 2007: The Missing Manual by E.A. Vander Veer

Premiere Elements 8: The Missing Manual by Chris Grover

QuickBase: The Missing Manual by Nancy Conner

QuickBooks 2010: The Missing Manual by Bonnie Biafore

QuickBooks 2011: The Missing Manual by Bonnie Biafore

Quicken 2009: The Missing Manual by Bonnie Biafore

Switching to the Mac: The Missing Manual, Leopard Edition by David Pogue

Switching to the Mac: The Missing Manual, Snow Leopard Edition by David Pogue

Wikipedia: The Missing Manual by John Broughton

Windows XP Home Edition: The Missing Manual, Second Edition, by David Pogue

Windows XP Pro: The Missing Manual, Second Edition, by David Pogue, Craig Zacker, and Linda Zacker

Windows Vista: The Missing Manual by David Pogue

Windows 7: The Missing Manual by David Pogue

Word 2007: The Missing Manual by Chris Grover

Your Body: The Missing Manual by Matthew MacDonald

Your Brain: The Missing Manual by Matthew MacDonald

Your Money: The Missing Manual by J.D. Roth

Introduction

Maybe a Facebook invitation showed up in your email inbox and you're trying to decide whether to join the site. Maybe you were alarmed when you heard your kids mention **poking** each other on Facebook. Maybe the Wall Street buzz caught your attention when Facebook—a whippersnapper of a website that didn't even exist until 2004—clocked in at a breathtaking value of $15 **billion**. Or maybe you caught the blockbuster movie (based on a bestselling book) about Facebook's founder, or noticed that Facebook mentions are regularly making it into your favorite local and national news programs.

However you heard about it, everybody seems to be talking about Facebook. And for good reason: In an astonishingly short period of time, Facebook has grown from an online yearbook for college kids to an Internet juggernaut with an estimated 500 million members.

So what *is* Facebook, anyway? It's a free-to-use, wildly popular *social networking site*—which just means it's a way to connect with other people—that combines the best of blogs, online forums and groups, photo sharing, and much more. By tracking the connections its members make with each other, Facebook makes it easy to find and contact people—everyone from old friends and roommates to new customers, new bosses, and even folks you've never met before who share your interests.

 Note If you're thinking that Facebook sounds a lot like MySpace, you're right. The difference? In a word, positioning. Facebook does pretty much the same stuff as MySpace, but in a cleaner, more controlled, more professional way. MySpace's blinking, flashing, online teen haven now boasts far fewer members than Facebook. And over half of all new Facebook members count themselves among the 25-and-older crowd, so it's not just for college kids anymore.

How Facebook Works

First, you type in your personal and professional information—as much or as little as you're comfortable sharing. (Most folks add extras such as photos and video clips.) Then, you establish connections with groups of Facebook members, like everybody who went to your alma mater, or everybody who works at your company. Finally, you add individual connections to other members, such as the guys on your soccer team, your next-door neighbor, and the two or three old flames you're still speaking to. Bingo: instant access to the personal and professional details of all the folks you're connected to, the folks *they're* connected to, and so on. You can think of Facebook as a 500-million-plus-entry searchable Rolodex—on steroids.

The two parts of the site you interact with most often are:

- **Your profile**. Your profile is the page that other Facebook members—friends, relatives, coworkers, long-lost roommates, potential bosses, and so on—see when they look you up on Facebook (you can, of course, view your own profile, too). The *Wall* part of your profile makes it easy for your friends to see what you're up to. The figure below shows a sample profile.

- **Your Home page**. The majority of your Facebook Home page is taken up by a *News Feed* that chronicles your friends' Facebook activities. The right side of the page shows stuff you might want to act on: upcoming events, requests your friends have made, suggestions for new friends, and so on. To get to your Home page, click either the word "facebook" or "Home" at the top of any Facebook screen.

What You Can Do on Facebook

Like all social networking sites, Facebook blurs the line between personal and professional: Your boss is just as likely to be on Facebook as your kids. Still, most folks focus on either professional or personal stuff when they're on the site. The following sections list some of the things you can do on Facebook.

Social Activities

Facebook began as a social networking site for college kids (it was started by a Harvard student), and personal interactions are still the main reason people sign up. On the site, you can:

- **Look up (and be looked up by) long-lost pals**. Facebook wouldn't be very useful if no one used their real names—you wouldn't be able to find anybody! But since it's fun to find people and have them find you (and because Facebook's official policy requires truthfulness), members tend to provide their real names, photos, and personal details. Chapter 3 teaches you how to search for people on Facebook.

- **Make new friends**. Facebook makes it easy to search out and contact folks with similar interests, whether you like Pedro Almodóvar movies or are frustrated with Geometry 102. And because your personal info is available for other Facebook members to see, you can learn a little about someone before you decide to contact or befriend him. Online special-interest *Groups* (Chapter 6) let you exchange views with like-minded Facebook members, and *Events* (Chapter 7) let you arrange face-to-face meetings with other members.

 Note You get to control how much regular, garden-variety, not-yet-friends-with-you Facebook members can see about you, and vice versa (Chapter 13).

- **Keep in touch with far-flung friends and family**. Other Facebook members can sign up for regular updates from you. For example, you can send out party updates to fellow students stuck in study hall, or share photos of your new granddaughter. Likewise, you can sign up to get updates about what your friends and family members are doing. Chapter 5 teaches you all about automatic updates.

- **Make yourself heard**. Facebook's blogging feature (called *Notes*— see page 97) lets you put text and photos on your profile. Think of it as a beefed-up online journal.

- **Play games**. Gaming is a big part of the site. According to Facebook, more people play games through the site than through Wii, Xbox, and PS3 put together. Check out Chapter 12 for tips on finding and playing Facebook games.

 Right now, you play games on Facebook by installing game applications (Chapter 12). However, rumor has it that Facebook will soon come out with a special website devoted to games called a gaming *portal*.

- **Buy and sell stuff**. *Marketplace* (Chapter 8), Facebook's answer to classified ads, lets you buy and sell stuff online using a credit card.

- **Keep tabs on your kids**. Facebook started out as a way for students to meet online, and it's still big with college and high-school kids. Getting acquainted with Facebook not only helps you understand the language your kids are speaking; it also gives you a frank look into their online social lives.

Professional Uses for Facebook

You don't have to be out of work to benefit from social networking. While business-oriented social networks like LinkedIn may be more popular with serious get-ahead types, more and more professionals are turning to Facebook to mingle, headhunt, advertise, and work together effectively. Here are some of the work-related things you can do on Facebook:

- **Find a gig**. The resumé you post on Facebook can be as extensive as you want (headhunters use Facebook, too), and there's always the want ads in Facebook's *Marketplace* (Chapter 8). But because jobs often go to the best-qualified friend-of-a-friend, Facebook's ability to show you who's friends with who can be even more useful—maybe one of your friends knows the hiring manager, say.

- **Find an employee**. Facebook can help you recruit—and even vet— new hires (see Chapter 9).

- **Keep up-to-date on team projects**. Subscribing to *feeds* (page 92) and *Notifications* (page 88) keeps you in the loop regarding upcoming deadlines and other details, such as whether team members on the other side of the building are still online or have left for the day.

- **Collaborate**. Use Facebook's *Walls* (page 78), *Notes* (page 97), and *Groups* (Chapter 6) to exchange ideas, photos, and more; *Messages* (page 69) to send email; and *Events* (Chapter 7) to schedule meetings and lunch dates.

- **Market yourself, your products, or your company**. For relatively little scratch, Facebook gives you a couple ways to promote things:

  — **Pages** are special, interactive profiles for companies, bands, celebrities, and nonprofit organizations that you can create for free.

  — **Ads** can include graphics and text; they appear in Facebook's ad space (the lower-right part of any screen).

  Big-bucks sponsor companies have even more marketing options. Chapter 11 explains all your choices.

About This Book

Facebook is a terrifically fun and useful site, and compared to a lot of other websites, it's remarkably easy to use. But that's true only *if* you already know what you want to do on Facebook, and—most important—why.

That's where this book comes in: It's the book you *should* have been able to download when you registered for Facebook. It explains what kinds of things you can do on the site and how to go about doing them. You'll find tips for diving headfirst into Facebook without looking like a newbie, keeping in touch with your friends, expanding your social circle, and using Facebook as a poor-man's business-collaboration tool. This book also guides you through the staggering forest of privacy options so you can get the most out of Facebook with the least amount of risk (see Chapter 13).

This book is designed for readers of every skill level, from I-just-plugged-in-my-first-computer-yesterday to Internet expert. Concise intros lead you into step-by-step instructions of how to get stuff done. The Notes scattered throughout the text give you alternatives and additional info, and the Tips help you avoid problems.

Missing Manuals on Facebook

You can find Missing Manuals' own home on Facebook by typing *Missing Manuals* into the Search box at the top of any Facebook screen. Use the Page's *Wall* (page 78) or click the Boxes tab and use the Page's *discussion board* (page 174) to post feedback about this book or any Missing Manual.

And the Page is a great place to meet other folks who are fans of Missing Manuals—or to declare that you like the series, too!

About MissingManuals.com

At *www.missingmanuals.com*, you'll find articles, tips, and updates to *Facebook: The Missing Manual*. In fact, we invite and encourage you to submit such corrections and updates yourself. In an effort to keep this book as up-to-date and accurate as possible, each time we print more copies of it, we'll make any confirmed corrections you've suggested. We'll also note such changes on the website, so that you can mark important corrections into your own copy of the book, if you like.

Also, on our Feedback page, you can get expert answers to questions that come to you while reading this book, write a book review, and find groups for folks who share your interest in using Facebook. And don't forget to check out this book's Missing CD page, which includes a clickable list of all the web addresses mentioned here. Head to *www.missingmanuals.com/cds* to find it.

We'd love to hear your suggestions for new books in the Missing Manual line. There's a place for that on MissingManuals.com, too (*www.missingmanuals.com/feedback*). And while you're online, you can also register this book at *www.oreilly.com* (you can jump directly to the registration page by going here: *http://tinyurl.com/yo82k3*). Registering means you'll be eligible for special offers like discounts on future editions of *Facebook: The Missing Manual*.

Safari® Books Online

 Safari® Books Online is an on-demand digital library that lets you easily search over 7,500 technology and creative reference books and videos to find the answers you need quickly.

With a subscription, you can read any page and watch any video from our library online. Read books on your cellphone and mobile devices. Access new titles before they're available for print, and get exclusive access to manuscripts in development and post feedback for the authors. Copy and paste code samples, organize your favorites, download chapters, bookmark key sections, create notes, print out pages, and benefit from tons of other time-saving features.

O'Reilly Media has uploaded this book to the Safari Books Online service. To have full digital access to this book and others on similar topics from O'Reilly and other publishers, sign up for free at *http://my.safaribooksonline.com*.

Chapter 1
Getting Started

oogle, the iPod, spam: Only a handful of technological forces have gone from tiny to towering seemingly overnight, and Facebook is part of this elite group. There's one big reason: Setting up a Facebook account couldn't be easier. In the time it takes to say "howdy," you too can be part of the frenzy.

Then—if you like—you can fill out an optional Facebook *profile*, a series of questions regarding your likes, dislikes, educational and professional background, and so on. You can even include photos of yourself. The more accurately and completely you describe yourself to Facebook, the more useful you'll find the site. (After all, headhunters and old college buddies can't find you if you fake your information.) This chapter shows you how to sign up for an account, fill out your profile, and get to your personalized Facebook Home page.

> **Tip** Of course, the more info you give Facebook, the greater the risk that someone will steal or misuse that information. See Chapter 13 for ways to get the most out of Facebook while minimizing your risk.

Signing Up for an Account

Facebook accounts are free, and have only two requirements: You need a working email address, and you have to be over 13 years old. Here's how to sign up:

1. **Point your web browser to *www.facebook.com.*** If you're on a Windows computer, you'll get the best results with Internet Explorer or Firefox. If you're on a Mac, use Firefox or Safari. (If you're not familiar with Firefox [it's free], check out *www.firefox.com*.)

Tip You probably don't want to sign up for Facebook using your cellphone because there's quite a bit of typing involved, but you can in a pinch; see Chapter 14 for details.

2. **In the Sign Up area, fill out all the fields**. Facebook doesn't let you skip any fields, but you can change your answers later (page 19).

   — **First Name/Last Name**. Facebook expects you to use your real name, not an alias. Don't type in the name of a group or company, and don't include special characters like parentheses or titles such as Mr., Ms., or Dr.

If you like, after you finish the sign-up process you can add your maiden name to your account so people you knew before you got hitched can find you. To do so: At the top of any Facebook page, click the Account link and click Account Settings on the drop-down menu. On the page that appears, click Name and type your full maiden name in the Alternate Name field. You'll see that Facebook is already set up to include your maiden name on your profile and in search results should any old flame be looking for you. Click the Change Alternate Name button when you're done.

 Tip For the most part, it's up to you whether or not you give Facebook accurate personal details. But Facebook actually uses a combination of computer programs and real, live humans to weed out obviously bogus registration details. Type in *Elvis Presley*, *Mickey Mouse*, or *The Joad Family* for your full name, for example, and there's a good chance your registration won't go through.

— **Your Email**. Make sure you type in a working email address. If you don't, you won't receive the confirmation message Facebook sends you, and therefore won't be able to complete the sign-up process. If you're interested in joining your employer's or school's Facebook *network* (see Chapter 2), use your work email address (*kris_kringle@acme.com*) or your student email address (*kris_kringle@asu.edu*), respectively. If you're worried about privacy, sign up for a free email address from a site such as *www.mail.yahoo.com* or *www.gmail.com* and give Facebook this new email address.

 Note Facebook limits you to one personal Facebook account per email address. If you're worried about losing access to your email account (and, therefore, to your Facebook account) you can add an alternate email address to your Facebook account; page 30 shows you how.

— **New Password**. Make up a six-character (or longer), case-sensitive password (you can use numbers, letters, and punctuation), and then jot it down in a notebook or some other safe place so you don't forget it.

— **Birthday**. Make sure the year you choose puts you over age 12— Facebook doesn't let under-13s use the site.

Facebook requires you to hand over your birth date when you're creating a personal account. But because not everyone wants to share her age with the world, the site gives you a way to hide your birth date from fellow Facebook members (see page 20).

When you finish, click the Sign Up button. If you forgot to fill out any of the fields, you'll see the Sign Up page again, this time with a message at the top that reads, "You must fill in all of the fields." If you filled everything in to Facebook's satisfaction, you'll see a second Sign Up page; here's what you do there:

— **Type the security check words into the "Text in the box" field**. This step is to make sure you're a real, live person and not a computer (computers can't read the squiggly text).

 If you wait too long to type in the words that appear above this field—say you get called away from your computer and leave the half-finished Sign Up page overnight—Facebook may refresh the words and ask you to type in the new ones.

— **Click the green Sign Up button**. Ideally, you should click both the Terms of Use link and the Privacy Policy link and read both of them *before* you click this button. In reality, though, you'd need 3 hours and a law degree to make sense of them. And because Facebook reserves the right to change them any time it gets the urge, you'd have to keep re-reading them every day. So just click Sign Up and be done with it. After you do, Facebook displays a three-step process you can use to find folks you know who are already on Facebook, and then describe yourself (by creating a Facebook *profile* and, optionally, uploading a picture of yourself) so that folks can find *you*.

Step 1: Finding Your Friends on Facebook

The whole point of being on Facebook is to get—and stay—in touch with people. So it's no big surprise that the first of Facebook's three setup steps gives you a chance to find out which of the folks you regularly email is already on Facebook. Page 50 covers this step in detail, but here's the gist:

1. **On the Getting Started screen, make sure Step 1: Find Friends is selected**.

2. **Click the name of the email account you use to communicate with the most pals (Yahoo, Windows Hotmail, or whatever) and then type in the email address you use with that account (and password, if there's a spot for it).** Or, alternatively, just leave in the email address you used when you registered for your Facebook account.

3. **Click the Find Friends button**. When you do, Facebook pops up a box asking you to log into your email account. (Or, if you're already logged into your email account, you may see a box asking you to confirm that it's okay for Facebook to access your friends' email addresses.) In either case, follow the instructions in the box and wait a second while Facebook scans your email account for email addresses and tries to match each one to a Facebook member profile.

Are your friends already on Facebook?

Many of your friends may already be here. Searching your email account is the fastest way to find your friends on Facebook.

Y! Yahoo!

Your Email: [redacted]

Find Friends

🔒 Facebook will not store your password.

Windows Live Hotmail   Find Friends

Gmail   Find Friends

Other Email Service   Find Friends

Skip this step

 Note If you don't use a web-based email address (such as *your_name@gmail.com,* *your_name@yahoo.com,* or *your_name@aol.com*), Facebook may not have any luck finding friends based on your address (you may even see an error message about the site being unable to import contacts from that address). In that case, just continue with the setup process and add friends later using the methods explained in Chapter 3.

If you regularly use email to keep in touch with pals *and* don't mind handing over the password to your email account (and that's a big if), the steps outlined above can be a quick way to add a bunch of your real-life friends to your Facebook social circle quickly and easily. But if you'd prefer to locate your friends on Facebook yourself after you've had a chance to create a profile (explained next)—or just don't feel comfortable giving email account info to Facebook—you've got options that you can come back to when you're ready, as Chapter 3 describes. For now, click the "Skip this step" link at the bottom of the page to move along and start building your profile.

Step 2: Creating Your Profile

A Facebook *profile* is a collection of facts about you: everything from where you went to school and how old you are to what kind of romantic relationship you're in (or hope to be in) and your favorite TV shows. All your Facebook friends and fellow network members can see your profile details (except for the Facebook members you explicitly exclude; see Chapter 13). Facebook automatically creates a bare-bones profile for you based on the info you entered when registering, and then gives you the opportunity to add just a couple more details concerning work and school that help you connect with Facebook friends quickly and easily. Whether or not you add additional details—and how much you add—is up to you.

 Tip If you *do* decide to flesh out your profile, brevity and truthfulness pay off by helping Facebook connect you with like-minded folks. That's because Facebook automatically lists your profile answers in other members' search results. The site can also suggest potential friends by matching your profile info with that of other members, as explained in Chapter 3.

When polishing your profile, ask yourself:

- **What do I want to get out of Facebook?** If you just want to check out your ex's Facebook profile, you don't need to waste time crafting one of your own. But if you hope to use the site to do some networking and land a job, spending time building your profile is definitely worth the effort.

- **How security conscious am I?** Although Facebook's success is based, in part, on its scrupulous commitment to member privacy, the sad truth is that everything you put on the Internet is subject to possible misuse and theft—including what's in your Facebook profile. So think twice about including political, religious, sexual, and other sensitive proclivities unless revealing these details is absolutely necessary. For example, if you registered for Facebook specifically to connect with other political activists in your area, fill out the political section of your profile; otherwise, skip it.

- **How much time do I want to spend on this?** Profile building can be a huge time-suck. If you're anxious to start using Facebook, just add a few details now. You can always add more later (page 19).

 Tip If all you add to your profile is one detail, make it a flattering picture of yourself (see page 15). Doing so is quick, easy, and lets folks who already know you identify you right off the bat—even if your name is John Smith.

To add basic school and work details to your Facebook profile:

1. **On the Getting Started screen, make sure Step 2: Profile Information is selected**.

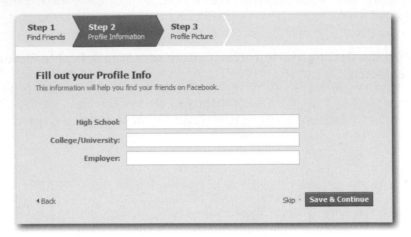

2. **Click in the High School field, start typing the name of the school you attended, and—when Facebook displays your high school's name—click to select it**.

3. **Repeat step 2 for the college or university you attended (or are attending) and the company you currently work for**. If you went to a bunch of colleges or have worked for a bunch of companies, you can list them all; page 27 tells you how.

4. **Click Save & Continue**. Facebook displays a list of members you might know based on the schools and workplace you selected. To *friend* (page 46) one or more of the folks listed, click the "Add as friend" link that appears below the person's picture. When you finish, click the Save & Continue button.

 Where you went to school and where you work are the most useful pieces of info to Facebook when it comes to matching you up with possible friends. To describe yourself more fully, flip to page 19.

If you'd rather not add anything at all to your profile at this point, click the Skip link at the bottom of the page. (You can always come back and add to your profile later; page 19 tells you how.)

Step 3: Adding a Picture of Yourself

Until you add a picture to your profile, Facebook displays a dorky blue-and-white outline of a person's head and shoulders. Replacing that outline with a picture of yourself is a good idea because it helps searchers identify you more easily. To add a picture to your profile:

1. **On the Getting Started screen, make sure Step 3: Profile Picture is selected**.

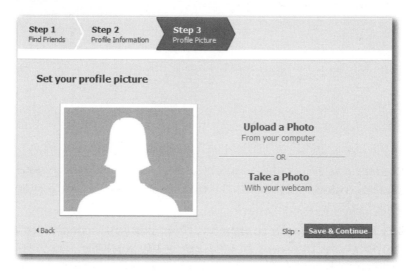

2. **Click the "Upload a Photo" link**.

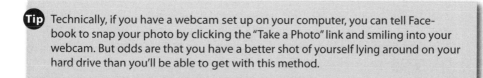

Tip Technically, if you have a webcam set up on your computer, you can tell Facebook to snap your photo by clicking the "Take a Photo" link and smiling into your webcam. But odds are that you have a better shot of yourself lying around on your hard drive than you'll be able to get with this method.

3. **In the Upload Your Profile Picture dialog box that appears, click Browse to search your computer for the 4-megabytes-or-less .jpg, .gif, or .png file you want to add to your profile**. After you select the picture you want, Facebook automatically adds it to your profile. (Page 22 shows you how to change it.)

Confirming Your Facebook Registration

After you register for an account, Facebook sends a confirmation email to the address you typed in during registration.

Most of Facebook's useful features (such as letting you join Groups and discussions) don't work until you confirm your registration, so you want to do so as soon as you get a chance. Here's how:

1. **At the top of any Facebook screen, click the "Go to your email" button that appears (it disappears after you finish confirming your registration), or just open your email program the way you usually do**. Either way, in your email program's inbox, you'll find a message from Facebook asking you to confirm that you want to join.

> **Tip** Facebook's pretty quick about responding to registration requests. Typically, the confirmation email shows up in your inbox within a couple of minutes.

2. **In your email program, click the link in the confirmation email or cut and paste the link into your web browser**. Bingo: Facebook displays a welcome message on your newly created, personalized Facebook Home page. Congratulations—you're officially registered! (You're automatically logged in, too.)

Viewing Your Profile

Taking a look at your profile from time to time is a good idea because it lets you see yourself as other Facebook members see you. To view your profile:

1. **Make sure you're registered (page 8) and logged in (page 31).** If you just finished registering by clicking the link in the confirmation email, you're already logged in.

2. **Head to the top of any Facebook screen and click Profile.** Your profile comes with three built-in sections to help organize your personal information: Wall (described on page 78), Info (which you use to update your profile information as explained in this section), and Photos (which you use to create and edit photo collections; see page 160). There are links to each of these sections on the left side of your profile page.

 Clicking the Friends link on the left side of your profile shows you your Facebook pals (Chapter 3).

The profile that appears lists all the info you've given Facebook. If you've just registered, the only details you see are the bare-bones ones Facebook got from you during the registration process.

 Note Until you tell Facebook differently, anyone on Facebook can see your profile (except for sensitive stuff like your birthday and your political and religious views, which only your friends—and their friends—can see). To fine-tune who can see what, head to the top right of any Facebook page and click the Account link, click Privacy Settings on the drop-down menu, and then, in the "Sharing on Facebook" section, either choose a quickie setting, such as "Friends of Friends", or click Customize to spell out exactly who you want to see which bits of information. Chapter 13 has the details.

3. **Click the Info link**. The Info section of your profile is divided into three sections: "Education and Work"; "Arts and Entertainment"; and Contact Information.

 Note If you've already added some profile info, you'll see that information listed in one of the three sections Facebook starts you out with.

4. **If you want to change anything listed on your profile, click the Edit icon that appears next to any of the three section headings.** (Alternatively, you can click the Edit Profile button on the far right of the screen.) When you do, nine categories of profile information appear on the left side of the screen: Basic Information; Profile Picture; Featured People; "Education and Work"; Philosophy; "Arts and Entertainment"; Sports; "Activities and Interests"; and Contact Information.

 Note Oddly, these nine categories don't match the three section headings that Facebook displays on your finished profile. Why is anyone's guess.

The following sections explain how to add to or edit your profile info.

 Tip If you have a blog, you may be able to save yourself some typing by putting a bunch of stuff on your Facebook profile and then—instead of retyping the same stuff on your blog—adding a clickable image called a *profile badge* to your blog. That way, when visitors to your blog click your profile badge, they shoot directly to your Facebook profile. To add a profile badge to an existing blog, click the "Add a Badge to Your Site" link that appears at the lower left of your Facebook profile (you may have to scroll down to see it). For details, see page 190.

Adding Basic Info

Most of the information Facebook lumps into this category really isn't all that useful. You'll probably just want to type in your hometown and city and skip the rest. (You can skip *all* of it, if you like; none of it's required.) Here's how to add this info to your profile:

1. **At the top of any Facebook screen, click the Profile link.**

2. **On the left side of the page that appears, click the Info link.**

3. **Click the Edit Profile button on the right side of the screen that appears.** Facebook displays a bunch of fields including Current City, Hometown, Sex, and Birthday.

 If you don't see these fields, head to the left side of the screen and make sure the Basic Information link is selected.

4. **Fill in as many of the following fields as you like:**

   — **Current City**. Start typing, and Facebook makes suggestions so you can select your city instead of typing its full name. Filling in this field is useful if you plan to attend in-person events advertised on Facebook (page 121).

   — **Hometown**. Filling this in can help long-lost pals identify you.

   — **Sex**. From the drop-down list, choose Male or Female.

 To keep "male" or "female" from appearing on your profile (which may help cut down the number of hey-baby-wanna-get-lucky messages you receive), turn off the "Show my sex in my profile" checkbox.

   — **Birthday**. If you accidentally entered the wrong date when you signed up, you can change it here. To hide your age or birthday from folks (and applications—see Chapter 12) who can see your profile, from the "Show my full birthday in my profile" drop-down list, choose "Show only month & day" or "Don't show my birthday".

Note Unless you plan to use Facebook as an online dating service, you can probably skip the next item.

- **Interested In**. If you're hoping to meet the love of your life on Facebook, create a wish list by turning on the checkbox next to the appropriate "Interested in" choice.

- **Languages.** If you speak seven languages and want all your friends to know, list the languages here.

- **About Me.** If you're dying to share information that Facebook doesn't have an official category for, this is your chance. You can type whatever you like in this field.

 Tip If you're planning to use Facebook to hunt for work, the About Me field is a great place to put your bio.

5. **When you're finished, click the Save Changes button at the bottom of the screen**.

Adding or Changing Your Profile Picture

Until you add a picture of yourself, your Facebook profile is about as visually appealing as a plain brown wrapper. You may have added a picture during the registration process (page 8). If you didn't—or if you did but want to change it—you can do so easily by creating or editing a Profile Picture Album containing multiple pictures, each of which you can give an optional caption.

 Tip Facebook lets you upload additional photo albums (page 161) and even *tag* the pictures you upload—including your profile picture. *Tagging* is a nifty way of assigning a portion of a picture to a specific Facebook member's name. For example, say you upload a shot of yourself that shows a coworker lurking in the background. You can click your own head and assign that portion of the picture to your name, and then click your coworker's head and assign that portion of the picture to her. Tagging helps Facebook members find pictures they're in, wherever those pictures appear—whether on a friend's profile or a mortal enemy's. For the skinny on tagging, check out page 166.

If you haven't uploaded a profile picture yet, here's how:

1. **At the top of any Facebook screen, click the Profile link.**

2. **On the page that appears, mouse over the placeholder picture and then click the "Change Picture" link that appears.**

3. **In the box that appears, click Browse to search your computer for the image file you want to add to your profile.** Make sure the image you choose is a .jpg, .gif, or .png file that weighs in at 4 megabytes or less (it probably will—these types of files tend to be pretty small). If you need help, the Tip on page 161 tells you how to check a file's type and size. After you select the file you want, Facebook automatically adds it to your profile. The next time you view your profile (page 17), you see your picture instead of the dorky silhouette.

If you've already added a picture to your Facebook profile and want to change it:

1. **At the top of any Facebook screen, click the Profile link and then, on the left side of the page that appears, click the Photos link.**

2. **On the page that appears, click the Profile Pictures album.**

3. **On the Profile Pictures page that appears, click the Change Profile Picture button**.

 Note You can click the tiny "Terms of Service" link on the next page that appears to read the legal nitty-gritty of what you're agreeing to, but here's the bottom line: Don't add a picture that you didn't personally shoot (or draw, or airbrush, or whatever).

4. **On the page that appears, click the Browse button to search your computer for the image file you want to add**. Choose a .jpg, .gif, or .png file that's smaller than 4 megabytes. After you make your selection, Facebook automatically uploads and displays your new picture.

Tip If you've already uploaded a bunch of pictures and simply want to swap out your current profile picture for another that you've uploaded previously: At the top of any Facebook screen, click the Profile link; then, click the Photos link on the left side of the next page. On the page that appears, click the picture you want to replace your current profile picture with (depending on how you've organized the photos you've already uploaded, you may have to click on an album first, and then a picture). On the screen that appears, scroll down and click the Make Profile Picture link and then, in the confirmation box, click Okay.

If you like, you can tweak your picture or add more images to your Profile Picture Album from this same page. Here are your options:

- **To upload an additional picture** to your Profile Picture Album, simply repeat steps 1–4.

- **To change your profile picture to another picture you've already added**, click the Profile link that appears at the top of every Facebook screen; then, on the upper-left side of the screen that appears, click your profile picture. Next, in the window that appears, click the photo you want. Finally, at the bottom of the window (scroll down), click the Make Profile Picture link and, in the confirmation box that appears, click the Okay button.

- **To add a caption to your profile picture**, click the Profile link at the top of any screen, and then click your existing profile picture in the upper left of the screen. On the Profile Pictures screen that appears, click the picture to which you want to add a caption, then scroll down below the picture and click the "Add a caption" link. In the field that appears, type your text and then click the Save button. (Captions appear when folks viewing your photo albums mouse over pictures.)

- **To delete a picture from your Profile Picture Album**, click the Profile link at the top of any Facebook screen. Then, on the upper-left side of the screen that appears, mouse over your profile picture, click the Change Picture link that appears, and then choose "Remove your Picture" from the drop-down list that appears.

Facebook displays a tiny thumbnail version of your profile picture in various places around the site depending on your Facebook activities. For example, if you join a *Group* (Chapter 6), Facebook includes your thumbnail in the Members section of the Group's profile page. And when you become friends with another member, your thumbnail appears on that person's *friend list* (page 61).

 Tip For a website that doesn't advertise itself as a photo-sharing site, Facebook lets you do a surprising amount of stuff to your pictures. You can organize them into albums, and easily share your pictures with Facebook members (and non-Facebook members, for that matter). You can even start a conversation about a particular photo by typing a comment alongside it—and encouraging others to do the same. To see your photo-sharing options, click the Profile link at the top of any Facebook screen, click the Photos tab, and then click the Profile Pictures link (or the link for any other photo album you've added to Facebook). On the page that appears, click any picture and then scroll to the bottom of the window.

Adding Relationship-Related Stuff

To describe your personal relationships on Facebook:

1. **At the top of any Facebook screen, click the Profile link**.

2. **On the right side of your profile page, click the Edit Profile button**.

3. **On the left side of the screen that appears, click the Featured People link**.

4. **Fill out as many of the following fields as you like:**

   — **Relationship Status**. Click this field to announce your availability (or lack thereof). If you choose a relationship that involves another person, Facebook pops up additional fields you can fill out or leave blank. For example, if you choose "Married," Facebook gives you the chance to fill in your anniversary and your spouse's name. (Bonus: If your spouse is also on Facebook, the site displays his or her profile picture.)

 Note If you decide to fill out the Relationship Status section of your profile, keep in mind that Facebook—like all communities, online and off—ascribes very specific meanings to what might seem like innocent labels. Choosing the status "It's Complicated" or indicating that you're "In an Open Relationship", for example, pretty much guarantees that sooner or later you'll receive the electronic equivalent of mash notes. (Adding provocative photos to your profile makes that even more likely, of course.)

   — **Family Members**. If any of your clan is on Facebook (or if you want them to be), you can list them here. This can be useful for organizing family reunions and remembering important birthdays. First, click the Select Relation field and then, from the drop-down list that appears, choose Son, Sister, or one of the other options. Then, in the blank field to the left of the Select Relation field and type in the person's name. To list more folks, click the "Add another family member" link and repeat the process.

   — **Featured Friends**. If you like, you can organize your friends into lists, such as "best friends," "work buddies," "out-of-town family," and so on. Doing so helps keep your worlds from colliding by making it easier for you to shoot the knock-knock jokes to, say, close friends without worrying about whether your mother-in-law or your boss will see them. To create a list, click the "Create new list" link, click the profile pictures of the friends you want to add to the list, and then click Create List. (If you're brand new to Facebook, you need to "friend" a few folks [see Chapter 3] before you can add those friends to a list.)

Adding Education- and Work-Related Info

If you're a student or work at a decent-sized company, adding a few school- or work-related details to your profile is well worth the time. After all, the whole point of Facebook is to try to mimic your real social circles—and if you're like most folks, a lot of your real-life friends are fellow students and coworkers.

You may have added basic school- and work-related info right after you registered for Facebook (page 8). Taking the time to add more details is handy for connecting not only with prospective employers, but also with long-lost pals, because Facebook lets you search for people based on matching profile info. So, for example, you can easily look up folks who worked at the same pizza place you waitressed at in college.

To add details about the school you go to (or attended in the past):

1. **At the top of any Facebook screen, click the Profile link and then click the Edit Profile button that appears at the top right of the screen**.

2. **On the left side of the screen, select the "Education and Work" link**.

3. **Fill out any of the following fields that appear (they're all optional):**

— **Employer**. When you start typing, Facebook displays a list of companies it knows about. If your company is among them, select it from the list; if not, just type in the name. In either case, as soon as you add an employer, Facebook pops up additional job-related fields.

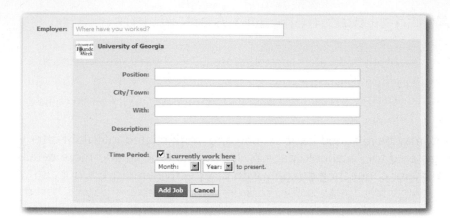

— **Position, City/Town, Description**. These are free-form fields where you can type whatever you like. If you expect to use Facebook for professional networking, make sure you load the Description field with accurate, descriptive, job- and industry-related buzzwords (think mini resumé).

— **With**. If you work (or worked) with a Facebook friend, you can type his name here.

— **Time Period**. Turn on the "I currently work here" checkbox if you're still at this job, and then click to select the month and year you started. If you leave this checkbox turned off, Facebook displays another set of Month/Year fields so you can enter the date you left the company.

 You can list up to five different employers/jobs by clicking the Add Job button that appears after you type in a job.

— **College/University**. As soon as you start typing, Facebook pops up a helpful list of schools you can choose from. You can add up to five different colleges or universities. Choose your graduation year from the Class Year drop-down list.

— **With**. If you attend (or attended) school with a Facebook friend, you can type her name here.

— **Concentrations**. Type in the subject you majored (or minored) in. You can add up to three different subjects.

— **Attended for**. Your choices are College or Graduate School.

— **High School**. Facebook lets you list up to two different high schools. Choose the year you graduated from the Class Year drop-down list.

4. **When you're finished, click Save Changes or Cancel**.

Adding Your Philosophical Views

If you click the Philosophy tab, Facebook displays the following fields (you can type as much as you like into any—or all—of them): Religion, Political Views, People Who Inspire You, and Favorite Quotations.

 Note Most of us were taught to be cautious about discussing religion and politics in public, and it's wise to consider everything you do on Facebook as taking place in public, because—even if you're scrupulous about adjusting and readjusting your privacy settings, as described in Chapter 13—mistakes happen. So unless you have a good reason for doing otherwise (maybe you joined Facebook to keep up with a specific religious or political group, say) you can probably skip the Political Views and Religious Views fields.

Adding the Stuff You Like and Do

Thanks to its roots as a souped-up yearbook for college students, Facebook encourages you to wax rhapsodic about such personal details as your hobbies and your favorite TV shows. To add that kind of info, follow these steps:

1. **At the top of any Facebook screen, click the Profile link**.

2. **On the right side of the page that appears, click the Edit Profile button**.

3. **On the left side of the screen, click "Arts and Entertainment."** On the page that appears, type as much as you like into any of the fields: Music, Books, Movies, Television, and Games.

 Tip Adding reams of personal tidbits—for example, typing a couple pages' worth of info into every field in the "Activities and Interests" section—marks you as a Facebook newbie.

4. **On the left side of the screen, click Sports**. On the page that appears, type as much as you like into the Sports You Play, Favorite Teams, and Favorite Athletes fields.

5. **On the left side of the screen, click "Activities and Interests."** On the page that appears, list your activities and interests (if you like).

6. **When you finish, click the Save Changes button and Facebook automatically updates your profile**.

Adding Contact Info

After you register, Facebook members can contact you several different ways, including sending you a message in Facebook and writing on your Facebook *Wall* (page 78). But if you like, you can give folks additional ways to contact you by listing your street address, phone number, and instant messaging screen names. Here's how:

1. **At the top of any Facebook screen, click the Profile link and then, on the left side of your profile page, click the Info link**.

2. **Scroll down to the Contact Information section and click the Edit link**.

3. **On the Contact Information page that appears, fill in as many of the following fields as you like**:

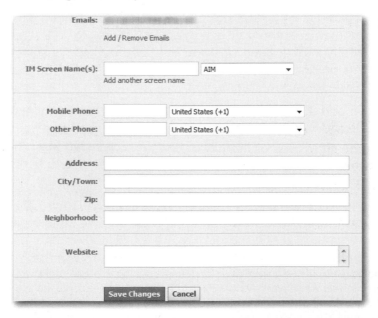

Right now, Facebook assumes you want your friends to be able to see your contact info, but because the site's privacy policy changes from time to time—and because controlling who gets to see your street address or cellphone number is a fairly big deal—you should double-check who can see that stuff. To do so, at the top of any Facebook screen, click the Account link and then click Privacy Settings on the drop-down menu that appears. On the Choose Your Privacy Settings page that appears, scroll down and click the tiny "Customize settings" link. Then, on the Customize Settings page, scroll down to the "Contact information" section and click the padlock icons next to Mobile phone, Address, or any other field. See Chapter 13 for details.

— **Emails**. Clicking the Add/Remove Emails link lets you change your contact email (the one Facebook uses to get in touch with you) and add alternate addresses.

If you're a glass-half-empty kind of person, you might want to add more than one contact email. Doing so gives you a backup way to access your Facebook account in case your primary email service goes down.

— **IM Screen Names**. If you have an account with an instant messaging service such as AIM (AOL Instant Messenger), you can add your IM alias or *screen name* to your account. Doing so lets anybody looking at your Facebook profile see if you're logged into your IM program (Facebook displays a green dot next to your screen name when you're logged in). If you are, people with an instant messaging program installed on their computers can click your screen name to start messaging you.

To add a screen name, type it into the field and then, from the drop-down list, select your instant messaging service. Your choices include AIM, Google Talk, Skype, Windows Live Messenger, and several others. Facebook lets you add up to five different screen names.

— **Mobile Phone, Other Phone, Address, City/Town, Zip, Neighborhood**. If you wouldn't feel comfortable heading to your local community center and tacking up a flyer listing your phone number and street address, you probably don't want to add these details to your Facebook profile.

— **Website**. You can list multiple websites; just make sure you type each web address—such as *http://www.mycoolsite.com*—on its own line. (Feel free to skip the *http://* part; Facebook adds it automatically.)

Tip If you want to give people who visit your website access to the info on your Facebook profile, click Profile and the top of any Facebook page, then scroll down and, in the lower-left part of the page, click the "Add a Badge to Your Site" link. Doing so whisks you to a Profile Badges screen displaying a clickable thumbnail image (which Facebook calls a *badge*) made up of your profile picture and the Facebook logo. Under the "Choose where to add the badge" heading, click the "Other" button. Then follow the onscreen instructions to cut and paste a bit of HTML code into one of your website's source files, and voilà—folks who visit your website can click on your badge to see your Facebook profile. If your website is a blog hosted by Blogger or Typepad, adding a Facebook badge is even easier; just click the appropriate button on Facebook's Profile Badges screen and then follow the instructions.

4. **When you're finished, click Save Changes**.

Viewing Your Facebook Home Page

After you've registered with Facebook, the site creates a Home page just for you. If you're already logged into Facebook, simply click the word "facebook" at the top left or the Home link at the top right of any screen to see your Home page. If you're not currently logged in:

1. **Point your web browser to www.facebook.com.** You see a generic welcome page with a spot for you to log into Facebook on the right.

2. **Log in.** If you always access Facebook from the same computer, you may find that your email address already appears in the Email field. If not, type in the email address and password you gave Facebook when you registered, and then click the Login button.

Tip Think twice before turning on the "Keep me logged in" checkbox. If you do, your browser will stay logged into Facebook until you specifically remember to log out. If you forget to log out, family members, coworkers, fellow library patrons, or anyone else who uses the computer after you log into Facebook can access your account.

Facebook takes you to your Home page, which includes a list of links on the left hand side, a News Feed section in the middle, and various info about Events (Chapter 7), requests, and other happenings on the right side (along with a bunch of ads). Think of this page as your Facebook control center: It gives you an overview of what your friends are doing and what you can do.

3. **After you finish your Facebook session, click the Account link in the upper-right part of any Facebook screen and then select Logout.** Doing so prevents other folks from getting into your profile and designating you as being "In an Open Relationship," say.

Changing Account Info

Some of the stuff you share with Facebook—like your password, for example—isn't for public consumption. Because these details are between you and Facebook, they're not part of your profile, but *are* part of your Facebook account. To change your account details:

1. **At the top of any Facebook screen, click the Account link and, in the list that appears, click Account Settings.** On the screen that appears, make sure the Settings tab is selected.

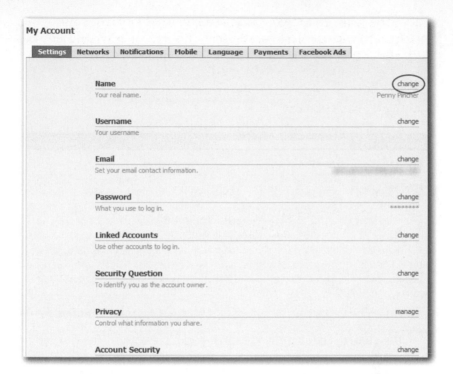

2. **Click the "change" link to the right of one or more of the following headings:**

— **Name**. If your name changes after you register with Facebook—due to a marriage or divorce, for example—you can update it instead of canceling your membership and re-registering. One caveat: Because Facebook runs your name change through security checks to spot potential fraud, the change won't take effect immediately. (Think days, not hours.)

— **Username**. Confusingly, usernames have nothing to do with the name you give Facebook when you register for an account, and they don't appear anywhere on your profile. In Facebook parlance, a *username* is an optional name you can use to make the web address people see when they pull up your Facebook profile look neater. For example, say your brother heads to your Facebook profile. In his browser's address bar, he sees something like this: *http://www.facebook.com/#/profile.php?ref=profile&id=100000598910304*. But after you choose a username, he'll see something like this instead: *http://www.facebook.com/YourName*.

At the time of this writing, you need to verify your Facebook account using a mobile phone in order to snag a username. For details on setting up a mobile phone to use with Facebook, check out page 237; for more on usernames, head to *www.facebook.com/username*.

— **Email**. If your email address changes, here's where you let Facebook know.

 Depending on how much you use Facebook, your inbox might be swamped with emails telling you that so-and-so wrote on your Wall or invited you to play virtual poker. Or, your email inbox might be under control, but the thought of your boss reading some of your old college buddies' Wall posts has you wishing for a way to keep your business and personal lives from colliding online. If either of these situations applies to you, consider getting a new email address just for your Facebook account. You can get a free email address from sites like *www.mail.yahoo.com* or *www.gmail.com*.

— **Password**. For security reasons, you have to type in your old password, and then enter your new password twice.

— **Linked Accounts**. If you regularly use another site, such as Google or Yahoo, and then switch over to Facebook (hey, there are worse morning-coffee routines), you can save time by telling Facebook to log you in automatically each time you log into Google (or Yahoo, or MySpace, or one of the other sites listed here).

— **Security Question.** Typing a security question (and an answer containing more than five letters and/or digits) comes in handy if you lose access to your Facebook account and need to contact Facebook to prove you're the account owner. (Account hijackings are rare, but you can't be too careful.) Just make sure you jot down your answer and keep it somewhere safe; after you create a security question, you no longer see this option on your Settings tab, so you can't change it.

— **Privacy**. Facebook lets you decide who gets to see the info you share with the site. Privacy is a big issue with potentially nasty ramifications, so all of Chapter 13 is devoted to understanding and customizing your privacy settings.

— **Account Security**. Turning on the Legal Notifications setting in this section tells Facebook to shoot you an email or text message if your account is accessed by a computer or mobile device other than the ones you typically use.

— **Download Your Information**. Facebook tracks everything you do on the site: the pictures you upload, the notes and messages you send, and so on. Clicking this link lets you download a copy of all the activity on your Facebook account from the minute you signed up to right now. (You have to be patient, as it may take anywhere from a couple hours to a couple days before Facebook notifies you that your download is ready; you also have to prove to Facebook that you're you before they release the goods.)

Tip Downloading a blow-by-blow of everything you've done on Facebook is a double-edged sword. On one hand, it might be useful if, say, you want to check that you've removed all your wild party pictures before a big job interview. And if you're the type of person who keeps important phone numbers on Facebook and you drop your cellphone in a lake, a Facebook download might just save your bacon. On the other hand, the download file you receive contains what most people consider super-private information, so you want to keep very close tabs on it.

— **Deactivate Account**. If you don't like Facebook, you can just stop using it, but Facebook gives you a better way to break things off. By *deactivating* your account, you get a chance to tell Facebook's designers why you don't like it (actually, you can't deactivate until you *do*). And turning on the "Opt out of receiving future emails from Facebook" checkbox during the deactivation process lets you stop Facebook-related notifications and invitations from appearing in your inbox.

Chapter 2
Joining a Network

What Facebook does best is track connections between people who've joined the site. The easiest way to make a bunch of Facebook connections in one fell swoop is to join a *network*—a group of people who have work or school in common: in other words, fellow employees at a company or graduates and current attendees of a particular school. Joining a network takes a lot of the grunt work out of finding interesting real-world groups and events, shopping for local stuff, and contacting real-life friends and coworkers. You can't just join any ol' network, though—there are some restrictions, as this chapter explains. And if you want to *create* a new network, you can suggest it to Facebook. Read on for the full scoop.

> **Note** Facebook used to let you join regional networks based on where you live, but a while back the company decided that these networks weren't worth the trouble and pulled them. After all, it's unlikely you're friends with everyone in your town just because they happen to live near you. So no more regional networks on Facebook.

How Networks Work

A Facebook *network* is simply a group of people who work or go to school (or who *used to* work or go to school) in the same place. You'll probably want to join at least one network as soon as you register, because until you do, the only folks whose profiles you can see are those you specifically tell Facebook you want to be friends with (see Chapter 3).

 Note You can't see a network member's profile until you join that network, but you *can* see a few public details, such as the member's profile pictures and friends.

When you join a network, two things happen:

- **You get immediate access to the Facebook profiles of all fellow network members, as well as access to the network's Groups, Events, market listings, and other goodies**. However, there are a few exceptions: Some Facebook members choose to hide their profiles, and some Groups and Events are restricted (see Chapter 13). But you still get access to a mountain of dishy details—all of which are potentially useful and interesting to you because you have something big in common with all the other network members: the school you go (or went) to, or the company you work (or worked) for.

 Note Another way to home in on people who share a common interest (such as Oprah fans, marathon runners, or needle felters) is by joining a Facebook *Group*. See Chapter 6 for the skinny.

- **Everybody else in the network can look up your profile information**. Network members can also see your hometown, your political views, your contact email address, and everything else you added to your profile (unless you've adjusted your privacy settings to explicitly exclude folks; see page 220).

Viewing the Networks You're Already On

Maybe you've already joined a network. Maybe you can't remember if you have or you haven't. To see which networks you've already joined:

1. **At the top right of any Facebook page, click the Account link and, in the drop-down list that appears, click Account Settings.**

2. **On the My Account screen that appears, click the Networks tab.** The tab that appears lists all the networks you belong to. To see who else is in a particular network, scroll down to the network you're interested in and click the "XYZ people" link.

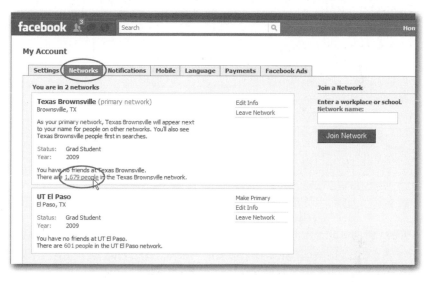

 Note Facebook automatically adds the *Global network* (see the next section for info on this unexclusive club) to everybody's account, but it doesn't appear in your list of networks or anywhere else. Like air, the Global network simply exists.

Joining a Network

When you register, Facebook automatically adds you to the not-super-useful Global network, which gives you access to globally organized groups and events. But you definitely want to join at least one more network. Technically, you can belong to as many as five different networks, but if you're like most people, two or three (a network for your work, your school, and maybe that fresh-out-of-college gig you left a few years back) fills the bill.

You can't just join any old network—you need a valid email address that matches the workplace, college, or high school network you want to join. For example, if your email address is frank_furter@ibm.com, Facebook lets you join the IBM workplace network. Or if your email address is guy_wire@asu.edu, you can join the Arizona State University college network.

Fortunately, you're not limited to one email address (and therefore one network). You can join multiple networks as long as you have multiple valid email addresses—for example, an address from the school where you got your undergrad degree, one from the school where you earned your master's, and one from your employer. To join multiple networks, follow the steps in this section, once through for each email address.

 Note If you join more than one network, you need to designate one as your *primary network*, which is the one that appears below your name when folks search for you. Because it represents the group you most closely identify with, it affects your search results (all other things being equal, Groups, Events, and Facebook members in your primary network appear in your search results first) and also affects the ads you see on the site.

To join a network:

1. **At the top right of any Facebook page, click the Account link and, in the drop-down list that appears, click Account Settings.**

2. **On the My Account page that appears, click the Networks tab.**

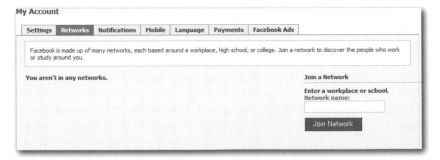

3. **In the "Network name" field, start typing the name of a school or company and, when Facebook displays the network you want, click to select it (you may have to click through the alphabetical list to find the one you want).** If the school or company name is really long, you can save yourself a little typing by entering the city where the school or company is located instead; when you do, Facebook pops up a helpful list of suggestions.

 Note High school networks don't work the same as other Facebook networks. The biggest difference is that you can't join a high school network using the steps in this list. Instead, when you register for Facebook—using either a valid high school email address or by responding to an invitation from a Facebook member who goes to your high school—Facebook automatically plops you in the correct high school network. If you're not using a valid high school email address, you have to be confirmed by a handful of friends—other Facebook network members who can vouch that they know you and that you attend the high school that matches your email address—before Facebook will let you in. And you can only switch high school networks once every 6 months.

4. **Depending on whether you're joining a school or company network, type in your work email address or your school status (undergrad, grad, or faculty), school year (when you graduated), and school email.** You need to have a company-issued email address to join a company's network, and a school-issued email address to join a school's network.

Tip If you've already graduated, no sweat: Alumni email addresses work, too. If you don't have one, contact your college to see if you can wrangle one. And if you don't see your company or school listed, you can ask Facebook to add it to its network list (see page 43).

5. **Click the Join Network button.** If the email address you typed in step 4 matches the company or school you chose, Facebook sends a confirmation message to that address. (If the address doesn't match, Facebook displays an error message.)

A confirmation email has been sent. Follow the confirmation link in that email.

6. **Open your favorite email program, find the network confirmation message Facebook sent, and follow the instructions in the email to confirm that you are who you say you are and that you really do want to join the network.** Now when people search for you on Facebook, your network appears under your name.

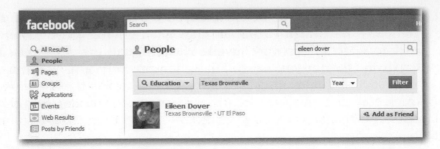

7. **If you like, join additional networks (you can have up to five total).** To do so, simply follow steps 3–6 for each network.

8. **If you join more than one network, tell Facebook which one you want to be your primary network.** Facebook automatically earmarks the first network you joined as your primary network, which means that when folks search for you on Facebook, they see this network listed under your name. (Your choice of primary network also affects *your* search results, because Facebook sorts them starting with the ones that match your primary network.) If the first network you joined isn't the one you feel is most "you," change your primary network. To do so: On the Networks tab of the My Account page, find the network you want to be your primary one and click the Make Primary link to the right of its name. Then, when Facebook kicks up a confirmation box, click the Make Primary button.

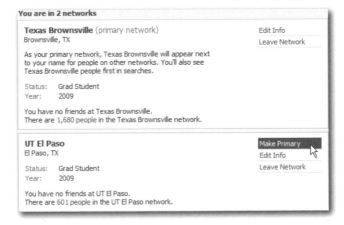

Leaving a Network

If the CEO of your company gets hauled into court on fraud charges and you're suddenly not so thrilled about people knowing where you work, you might want to drop your work network. You can leave any (or all) of the networks you join; just be aware that when you do, you forfeit the right to see your fellow network members' profile details and participate in network-related Events and Groups. To leave a network: On the Networks tab of the My Account page, scroll down to the network you want to jettison and click the Leave Network link to the right of its name. In the confirmation box that appears, click the Leave Network button. You're outta there!

Suggesting a New Network

Maybe you work for a small company or went to school in a tiny backwater town. If you check Facebook's network listings and don't see a network that describes where you work or go to school, you can ask Facebook to add your school or company to its network listings. Just follow these steps:

1. **Point your web browser to one of the following**:

   — **For work networks**: *http://www.facebook.com/help/contact.php?show_form=add_work*

   — **For college networks**: *http://www.facebook.com/help/contact.php?show_form=add_college*

   — **For high school networks**: *http://www.facebook.com/help/contact.php?show_form=hs_add*

 Tip To save yourself from typing all that gobbledygook, head to this book's Missing CD page at *www.missingmanuals.com*, where you'll find a clickable list of all the links mentioned in this book.

2. **Fill out the fields that appear and, when you finish, click Submit**. Because actual people need to approve your request, expect to wait a few days—or even weeks—for Facebook to get back to you. There's no guarantee they'll approve your request, but if your network suggestion is reasonable, you'll probably get a thumbs-up.

Chapter 3
Finding and Adding Friends

In real life, your social network consists not just of people who work or study where you do, but also of people you've formed one-on-one relationships with: teachers, ex-sisters-in-law, bowling buddies, and so on. It's the same with Facebook: You start with a network of school or work buddies (see Chapter 2), and then add friends one at a time. You can also use Facebook to look up old friends and find new ones.

Why would you want to enlarge your Facebook social circle? Well, having friends is really the whole point of joining Facebook. You get to swap life-in-progress tidbits (both serious and silly), share what you're reading, play online games…the list is endless. But first you need to gather your pals. Read on to learn how.

How Facebook Friends Work

In the world of Facebook, a *friend* is any Facebook member who has agreed that you two have something in common. Maybe you play on the same softball team, volunteer at the local animal shelter together, or keep running into each other at parties thrown by the same ex-roommate. Maybe you dated, took a road trip together, or you're second cousins twice removed. How you know a Facebook friend doesn't matter; all that matters is that you *both* agree that you know each other.

 Note Facebook has no way of verifying the relationships between friends. But one of the major differences between Facebook and MySpace—the other big social networking site—is that Facebook strongly encourages truthfulness. So, while having a zillion "friends" is considered a status symbol on MySpace, it's not such a big deal on Facebook—and may even prove annoying. Because Facebook lards your home page with news of your "friends'" activities, having to weed through a bunch of news about people you don't really know doing a bunch of things you don't really care about gets old quick. On Facebook, the goal is to put together a manageable list of people you actually know—and actually care about keeping up with.

Two people become Facebook friends when one person extends an invitation and the other person accepts, or *confirms*, it. When you become friends with someone on Facebook, three things happen:

- **You appear on your friend's *friend list* (page 61) and on her profile page (and vice versa).** On Facebook, as in life, you're known by the company you keep: Everyone with access to your friend's profile (or yours) can see the relationship between the two of you. And with the click of a mouse, folks can hop from your friend's profile to yours, or from your profile to your friend's.

 Note One of the best, most addictive things about Facebook is its confessional nature. Facebook *profiles* encourage members to pontificate about subjects that don't often come up in polite conversation. So, when you're friends with someone in Facebook, you might be surprised by the juicy details you learn about them.

- **You can see your friend's profile (and vice versa) even if he's not in your network**. This means you can see the Events he's planning to attend, the Groups he's joined, and all the other people he's friends with, among other details. (The exception to this is if your friend has specifically *blocked* you from seeing certain personal details, as explained on page 231.)

- **You receive automatic updates in your *News Feed* (page 84) chronicling your friend's Facebook activities (and vice versa)**.

 Tip Chapter 5 explains how to sign up for updates on your friends' Facebook activities and how to customize the updates your friends get about you.

Finding Friends

Before you can make someone your friend, you first have to find that person on Facebook. The site gives you four different ways to do this:

- You can look up real-life friends and acquaintances who are already Facebook members.

- You can invite real-life friends and acquaintances who aren't on Facebook to join the site.

- You can search for Facebook members you've never met but who share your interests (such as a background in server-side technology or a passion for container gardening).

- You can browse through the potential friends Facebook suggests for you (based on criteria such as both of you going to college at the same time and sharing a common Facebook friend).

The following sections explain all of your options.

Finding People Who Are Facebook Members

Some of your real-life friends and acquaintances might already be on Facebook. To find them, use one of the following search methods:

- **Search for Facebook members by name.** To do so:

    1. **Start typing the person's name in the search box at the top of any Facebook screen.**

    2. **If one of the profile pictures Facebook pops up looks like the person you're trying to find, bingo: You've found your pal!** Simply click her picture to see her profile. Otherwise, click the "See more results" link at the bottom of the list of suggested people.

    3. **On the search results page that appears, click the People link on the left-hand side to weed out extraneous results, such as Groups and applications that happen to contain your searchee's name.** Facebook displays a list of people matching the name you typed in. If the list is gigantic, you can narrow your search using the drop-down menu at the top of the list. Choose Location, Education, or Workplace from the menu, and then type a location, school, or workplace in the text box and click the Filter button.

Tip In Facebook, all clickable links are blue. If one of the names you see in your search results (or on your Friends List, or anywhere else in Facebook) is blue, then clicking it takes you straight to that person's profile (or as much of the profile as the person has granted you access to; see page 220).

- **Search for Facebook members who are classmates, ex-classmates, or coworkers**. At the top right of any Facebook screen, click the Account link and, from the drop-down list, choose Edit Friends. (If you've already added a friend or two, you need to take one extra step at this point: Head to the left side of the page that appears and click Find Friends.) Then scroll down and click the Other Tools link. When you do, Facebook displays a list of links customized based on the information you've provided to the site, so they'll read something like, "Find Classmates From [your high school]," "Find Classmates From [your college]," and "Find Coworkers From [your company]".

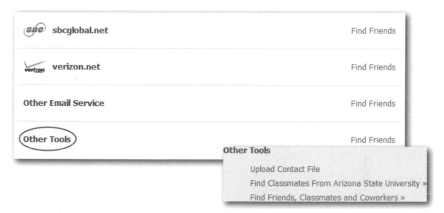

Note If you're new to Facebook, you'll see a "Find friends" link in the upper right of every screen, and a "Find people you know" link in the middle of your Home page (you may need to scroll down a bit to see it). Clicking either of these links takes you directly to the Find Friends page displaying a list of folks (along with ways to organize them to quickly find the ones you want to befriend).

The next screen that appears depends on which link you click and how many details you added to your profile. For example, if you already told Facebook you graduated from Arizona State University in 1990, then clicking "Find Classmates From Arizona State University" displays a list of members whose profiles mention that they attended ASU in 1990. If, on the other hand, you haven't added any work-related details to your profile and click the "Find current or past coworkers" link, Facebook displays a screen you can use to type in the company you want.

Search by Company

Company: _____

Person's Name: _____
(optional)

Search for Coworkers

- **Search for people you regularly email from your web-based email account**. If you have a web-based email address (such as *your_name@gmail.com, your_name@yahoo.com,* or *your_name@aol.com*), you can give Facebook your email account password and let it scan your email address book for matching Facebook members. Here's how:

At the top right of any Facebook screen, click Account, then choose Edit Friends; if you already have a few Facebook friends, you also need to click Find Friends on the left side of the Friends screen. (Alternatively, you can click the two-headed Friend Requests icon that appears to the immediate right of the Facebook logo in the upper left of any screen, and then click the Find Your Friends link that appears.)

In the Find Your Friends Wherever They Are section of the page that appears, simply click the email service you use to keep in touch with the most pals, type in your email address (and, if prompted, your email password so Facebook can access your email account), and then click the Find Friends button. If Facebook finds members who match the email addresses in your address book, it displays them; if it doesn't find any matches, it pops up a message box asking if you'd like to try a different web-based email account.

 Keep in mind that when you enter your email account password, you're handing over some pretty sensitive info to Facebook. After all, that password is the virtual key to your email account, your address book, and probably a bunch of other personal goodies. While Facebook is a reputable outfit and pledges not to store your password, you might want to skip this step if this whole sharing business makes you queasy.

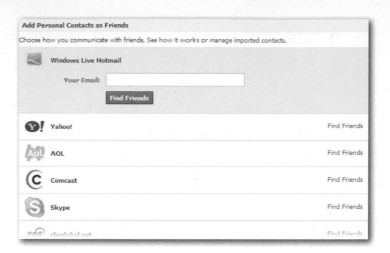

- **Search for people you regularly instant message**. If you use an instant-messaging program like AOL Instant Messenger (AIM), ICQ Chat, or Windows Live Messenger, you can add your IM screen name and password to your profile and then tell Facebook scan your buddy list for matching Facebook members. To do so: At the top right of any Facebook screen, click the Profile link. On the left side of your profile page, click the Info link, and then scroll down and click the Edit icon next to the Contact Information heading. In the IM Screen Names field, type your screen name, and then choose your messaging service (AIM, Skype, or whatever). When you finish, click the Save Changes button. Then, at the top left of your screen, click the Friend Requests icon (the silhouette of two people), and then click the Find Your Friends link. Scroll down the page that appears and click your instant messaging service (you won't see it unless you've already added a screen name to your profile). Finally, type in the screen name and password you use with your service and then click the Find Friends button. Facebook either displays matching Facebook members, or a message box asking if you'd like to try your search again (you don't; if Facebook didn't find any matches the first time, it won't find any the second).

- **Search for people you regularly email using a list of contacts**. Depending on the email program you use, you can export a list of email addresses from the program and let Facebook scan the list for matching Facebook members. (If you use a web-based email account, see page 50 instead.) To do so: On the right side of your Home page, click the "Find your friends" link (or, alternatively, at the top left of any screen, click the Friend Requests icon that's right next to the Facebook logo, and then click Find Your Friends). Scroll down the page that appears and click the Other Tools link, then click the Upload Contact File link. In the section that appears, either tell Facebook to scan your Windows/Outlook/Outlook Express contacts by clicking the "Find my Windows Contacts" button, or (if you use another email program, such as Mozilla Thunderbird or Mac OS X Address Book) click the "How to create a contact file…" link and then the name of the appropriate email program. Then follow the instructions you see to create and upload an email contact file Facebook can read. After you finish, click Find Friends. Facebook either displays the Facebook members whose email addresses match those on your list, or a link you can use to get technical help.

- **Leaf through the friend suggestions Facebook offers**. Facebook uses what it knows about you (based on your profile and any friends you've added) to come up with a helpful list of folks you may know: Facebook members who went to the same school at the same time you did, for example, or friends of people you're already friends with. These suggestions appear on the right side of your Home page under the People You May Know heading when you're new to Facebook, but you can also get to them by clicking Account at the top of any screen and selecting Edit Friends. On the left side of the screen that appears, click Find Friends, and then scroll down to the People You May Know section. To see more suggestions, click the More link. To tell Facebook to stop suggesting someone you know you'd never befriend in a million years (the ex-brother-in-law who dented your car that time and never made good, for example), click the tiny X next to the person's name.

Finding People Who Aren't Facebook Members

You can't add people to your friend list unless they're Facebook members. But say you've got a few real-life pals you wish would sign up for the site so you could keep in touch more easily. Facebook gives you an easy way to invite these people to join:

1. **On the right side of your Facebook Home page, find the Get Connected section (you may have to scroll down) and click the "Invite them now" link.**

2. **On the Invite Your Friends page that appears, type in your non-Facebook-pals' email addresses in the "To:" field, separated by commas; then type in a quick message (if you like) and click Invite.** Facebook sends invitations to all the addresses you listed.

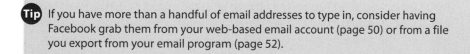

Tip If you have more than a handful of email addresses to type in, consider having Facebook grab them from your web-based email account (page 50) or from a file you export from your email program (page 52).

Finding New Friends

Back in the olden days of Facebook, the site gave its members an easy way to connect with each other one-on-one based on shared interests and other profile information, such as political views, hobbies, or favorite bands. You simply typed in what kind of folks you wanted to meet—for example, single moms in your area who like to knit—and bingo: You got an instant list of potential pals, complete with a built-in conversation opener.

You can still search for kindred spirits on Facebook—after all, that's one of the reasons Facebook is so popular—but to keep from becoming a giant spam free-for-all, the site has changed the way you search. Rather than the advanced search feature you used to use, Facebook now offers four different ways to find like-minded members:

- **Friend suggestions**. As you just learned, Facebook suggests folks you might be interested in being friends with based on criteria such as your profile details and the friends you already have. To see these suggestions, follow the steps on page 52.

- **Groups**. If you want to meet fellow history buffs or gardeners (or folks interested in any other topic or activity), Facebook's old *Groups* are a good place to start. To search through old Groups: At the top of any Facebook screen, type the topic you're interested in into the Search box, and then click the "See more results for [topic]" link that pops up. On the left side of the search results page that appears, click the Groups link to narrow your results.

You can find out more about Groups both old and new—including how to create a new one—in Chapter 6.

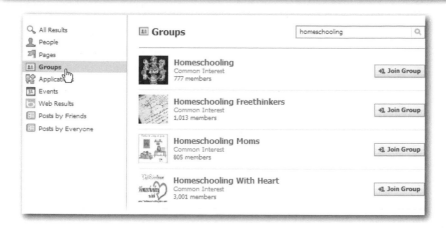

- **Keyword search**. Searching member details for a specific phrase or keyword, wherever it appears, isn't for the fainthearted (the phrase "like looking for a needle in a haystack" comes to mind). Still, depending on what kind of topic or activity you're searching for, it might yield good results. The more unusual the topic or activity, the better your chances of finding what you're looking for. To search member details: At the top of any Facebook page, type what you're looking for into the Search box and then click the magnifying glass icon on the right side of the box. On the left side of the search results page that appears, click the People link.

 If you decide to conduct a keyword search, prepare for a mountain of results. Also keep in mind that Facebook displays results no matter which member detail matches your keyword or what words or phrases surround it. For example, searching for "bears" will find both the guy who founded "Citizens Against Bears" and the lady who listed "The Zygote Bears" as her favorite band, among a zillion other results. To home in on Facebook members who live in a certain city, attend a certain school, or work at a certain company (based on their Facebook profiles), select Location, Workplace, or School at the top of the search results page, type in your criteria, and then click the Filter button.

- **Third-party search applications**. If you don't find what (or who) you're looking for using Facebook's search feature, you can try a search application (see page 197 for the scoop on Facebook applications). To find a search application: At the top of any Facebook screen, type *search* in the Search field, click the magnifying glass icon, and then click the Apps link on the left side of the screen that appears.

Note Facebook applications vary in quality, and they all look and work a little differently. So after you find one you think looks interesting, you'll want to spend a couple minutes checking out its reviews and playing with it to see if it works for you. To learn more about Facebook applications, flip to Chapter 12.

Inviting People to Be Your Friend

You can't just add people to your friend list willy-nilly; they have to be Facebook members *and* agree to be added. (Page 53 explains how to invite non-Facebook members to join the site.) To invite a Facebook member to be your friend:

1. **Search for the person you want to befriend (see page 54).**

Note If you send a friend request to someone who can't normally see your profile— she's not in your network, for example—Facebook temporarily grants that person access to the basic, work-related, and education-related portions of your profile (page 17) so she can make an informed decision about whether or not to accept your invitation.

2. **If your search returns the person you're looking for, click the "Add as Friend" button you see to the right of the person's profile picture.** Alternatively, click the person's name or picture to read a bit more about her and then, at the top of the potential friend's profile page, click the "Add as Friend" button. If you don't find the person you're looking for, you can invite her to join Facebook (page 53).

If you don't see the "Add as Friend" button, it's because the person you're trying to befriend has adjusted her privacy settings to block friend requests (see Chapter 13 for details).

3. **Fill out the confirmation box that appears and then click Send Request**. In the confirmation box, Facebook gives you the option of including a note along with your request; simply click the "Add a personal message" link. You may also see a couple of other options: If you've created any Friend Lists (page 63), you can click the "Add to List" button to add the person to a Friend List (assuming she accepts your request). And if you've activated your cellphone with Facebook (see page 237), you can turn on the "Subscribe via SMS" checkbox to have that person's posts sent to your phone.

After you click Send Request, you see a Friend Request Sent dialog box that lets you know Facebook has sent an invitation to your would-be friend's email address *and* posted a friend request to her Facebook Home page (page 31).

 If you're new to Facebook, the Friend Request Sent dialog box may include friend suggestions (friends of your soon-to-be-friend) for you to consider. Click "Add as Friend" if you're interested, or Close if you're not.

Note If the person you're extending the virtual hand of friendship to is brand-new to Facebook, after you send the friend request, Facebook displays a list of your current friends—just in case you want to ask them to join you in extending *their* virtual hands.

While you're waiting to hear back from your friend, a "Friend Requested" button replaces the usual "Add as Friend" button next to her name in your search results, and when you visit her profile, you see an "Awaiting friend confirmation" label next to her name. If your friend agrees to the friendship and responds either to the email or the Facebook request (page 50), Facebook adds your name to her friend list, and her name to yours. Facebook also sends you a *Notification* (see page 88) letting you know that she confirmed the friendship.

 Note In its quest to support polite social interactions, Facebook doesn't give members a way to explicitly reject friend invitations, but they *can* ignore them. If you've sent an invitation and haven't heard back after a few days, try sending the person a message or *poking* him (page 77). Still no answer? Sorry—you've been snubbed.

Responding to Friend Requests

When someone tries to add you to her friend list, two things happen: Facebook sends you an email invitation and posts a little notice on your Home page telling you that someone wants to be your friend. At that point, you've got two choices: You can confirm the request or ignore it, either on Facebook or right in your email program.

Confirming Email Requests

If you're the type of person who checks his email every hour (or every 5 minutes) but only logs onto Facebook every couple of days, you'll want to handle friend requests from inside your email program. Here's how:

1. **Look in your email inbox for a message with the subject "[Somebody] wants to be friends on Facebook."**

Hi Eileen,

Penny Pincher wants to be friends with you on Facebook.

Respond now:

Confirm Friend

Penny Pincher

Thanks,
The Facebook Team

To confirm (or quietly ignore) this request, go to:

2. **Open the message and click the green Confirm Friend button or the confirmation link**. Doing so whisks you to the Facebook page where you can confirm your friendship as explained in the next section.

Confirming Requests in Facebook

Some people log into Facebook whenever they're in front of a computer. If you're one of them, it's easier to respond to friend requests from your Facebook Home page than to fire up your email program and wade through your inbox looking for invitations. To confirm a friend request from inside Facebook:

1. **At the top of any Facebook page, click the Friend Requests icon just to the right of the word "facebook"**. The icon looks like the heads and shoulders of two little people (hover your cursor over the icons to see what each one is called). Above it, you'll see a red icon indicating how many friend requests you have. When you click it, Facebook takes you to the Confirm Requests page.

 Friend requests also appear on the upper-right side of your Home page under Requests. (If you don't have any friend requests, you won't see any listed under Requests.) Simply click the "friend request(s)" link there to view them.

2. **Make sure you want to accept the request, and then click Confirm**. After you click Confirm, you're Facebook friends with that person. Easy, huh?

Note If you've never heard of the person who sent you the friend request, the message he sent doesn't make sense, or the two of you have no friends in common, then you probably want to click the person's name and check out his profile (and perhaps send him a "Do I know you?" message by clicking the Send Message link that appears beneath his profile picture) to make sure the request is on the up-and-up.

 Tip To see what friends you and your new friend have in common, Facebook lets you know by displaying a "[number] mutual friend(s)" link after the person's name on the Confirm Requests page. Simply click this link or, on the right side of her profile page, click the Mutual Friends link to see the acquaintances you share.

Ignoring a Friend Request

In Facebook as in life, there will be times when someone extends the hand of friendship and you just don't want to shake it. After all, confirming a friend request doesn't only give your new pal (and all the Facebook applications he uses; see page 198) access to a big chunk of your personal life; it also lets the world know that you think enough of the guy to declare yourself his friend. If you get a friend request from someone you've never heard of, say, or whose profile paints a picture so creepy you want to lock your virtual door, all you have to do is quietly remove all traces of the request and get on with your life. To do so:

1. **Sign into Facebook (page 31) if you're not already there**.

2. **At the top of any Facebook page, click the Friend Requests icon just to the right of the word "facebook"**.

3. **On the screen that appears, click Not Now**. That's all you have to do: Facebook instantly removes the red number above the Friend Requests icon on your Home page.

4. **Back in your email program, delete the friend-request email**.

Viewing Your Friends

Facebook automatically displays 10 randomly selected friends on the left side of your profile (you may need to scroll down to see it).

To see more than these 10 friends—or to see more details about each of your friends—you've got a few options. You can:

- **See all of your friends in one fell swoop**. To do so:

  — On your profile page, click the Friends link that appears above the 10 random friends.

  — At the top right of any Facebook screen, click the word Account, and then click Edit Friends. On the Friends page that appears, click the Recently Interacted button and, from the drop-down list, choose All Friends.

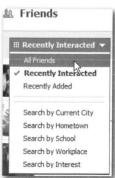

Tip The beauty and fun of Facebook lies in its who-knows-who connections, and the site makes it easy to play matchmaker. To suggest that a Facebook friend consider friending another of your pals: On one friend's profile page, scroll down until you see the Suggest Friends link on the left side of the page. Click the link and then, in the dialog box that appears, click to turn on the checkbox next to as many of your other pals as you like. When you finish, click Send Suggestions.

- **See friends who are online right this minute**. At the bottom right of any Facebook screen, the number that appears to the right of the word "Chat" tells you how many of your Facebook friends are currently logged into the site. (The word "Offline" may appear instead of a number.) Click the Chat link and a window pops up showing you exactly which of your friends are currently logged into Facebook.

> **Tip** To send a real-time chat message to a friend, in the Chat window, simply click the name of the person you want to chat with. A green dot means the friend is actively using the site (and so is probably going to see your message); a half-moon shape means the friend is logged into Facebook but hasn't done anything on the site for 10 minutes (and so may be out on a doughnut run). See page 76 for details on chatting.

- **See your friends organized by whether you know them from college, work, your area, or a common passion**. At the top right of any Facebook screen, click the word Account, and then click Edit Friends. On the Friends page that appears, click the Recently Interacted button and, from the drop-down menu, choose Search by Current City or Hometown (to see friends grouped by where they live now or used to live), School (to see friends who belong to college networks), Workplace (to see friends who belong to work-related networks), or Interest (to see friends who listed Chihuahuas, chili cook-offs, or some other interest on their profiles). If you've joined a network (page 37), the network's name appears in the drop-down menu, too; click it to show only those friends who belong to the same network.

> **Note** When you choose Search by Current City, Hometown, School, Workplace, or Interest, Facebook displays a text field you can use to indicate which particular city, school, company, or hobby you're interested in grouping your friends by.

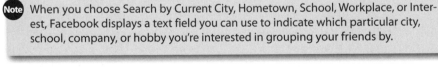

Organizing Your Friends

The options Facebook gives you for viewing your friends are great if you have only a handful of pals. But if you're a hardcore social butterfly with dozens or even hundreds of friends, you'll want to organize them into separate lists that reflect how you categorize them in your mind.

For example, imagine that in addition to your workplace network, you're involved in a book club, a softball league, and a 12-step program. Creating a separate list for each group of people lets you keep track of your different social circles at a glance. And because Facebook lets you send the same message to all the friends on a single list all at once (see page 65), control how much news about the list you want to see on your News Feed (Chapter 5), and even invite everyone on the list to join the same Group (Chapter 6) or Event (Chapter 7), creating separate Friend Lists helps you communicate with folks quickly and reduces the risk of having your worlds collide.

Creating a Friend List

Facebook lets you create up to 100 different Friend Lists, each of which can contain up to 1,000 names. (Of course, unless you're a politician, you probably won't need anywhere near that many.) Here's how to create one:

1. **At the top right of any Facebook page, click the Account link, and then click Edit Friends**.

2. **On the Friends page that appears, click the "Create a List" button**.

3. **In the "Enter a Name" field of the box that appears, type a name for your list and then hit Enter**. In the following example, the list's name is "out-of-town family".

4. **Add some friends to your list**. The easiest way is to click the thumbnail pictures of the people you want to add to your list. (Clicking a thumbnail once turns it blue to let you know you've selected it; clicking again deselects it.) Alternatively, you can click the "Start Typing a Name" field and type in names one at a time.

5. **When you finish, click the Create List button**. Your newly created list appears on the Friends page (click Account, then Edit Friends to get there) beneath the Lists heading. It also appears on your Home page (page 2) when you click the Friends link on the left-hand side of the screen. When you view thumbnail pictures of any of the friends you've added to the list, the list's name appears next to those people's names.

Tip You can add the same person to multiple Friend Lists.

Viewing a Friend List

To see all the people on a particular Friend List:

1. **At the top right of any Facebook screen, click the Account link and then click Edit Friends**.

2. **On the left side of the Friends page that appears, click the name of the Friend List you want to view**. Facebook displays the names and profile pictures of the friends you've added to that list.

If you want to see what everyone on a particular Friend List has been up to lately, head to your Home page by clicking the word "facebook" or "Home" at the top of any screen. On the left side of the screen, click the Friends link, and then click the name of the list you want to see. (If you have a lot of Friend Lists, you may need to click the More link to see them all.) Facebook shows you those friends' recent activities.

Editing a Friend List

Online or off, social circles and friendships change over time. After you've created a Friend List (page 63), you can change its name, add people to it, or delete folks from it.

To rename a list:

1. **Go to the left side of your Home page and click the Friends link**. Facebook displays all your Friend Lists below the Friends link.

2. **Click the name of the list you want to change**.

3. **On the page that appears, click the Edit List button**.

4. **In the dialog box that pops up, click the Edit link and then make your changes. When you finish, click the Save List button**.

 Note Alternatively, you can change the name of a Friend List by clicking the Account link at the top of any Facebook screen and then clicking Edit Friends. On the left side of the page that appears, click the name of the list you want to rename and then, at the top of the screen, click the Edit Name link and then follow step 4 above.

To add friends to an existing list:

1. **At the top left of any Facebook page, click the Account link and then click Edit Friends**.

2. **On the left side of the screen that appears, click the name of the list you want to add friends to**.

3. **Type someone's name into the "Type a friend's name to add" field (Facebook pops up a helpful list after you begin typing).** Alternatively, if you spot your friend's name in the Suggested For This List section on the right side of the list page, click the plus sign that appears next to that friend's name.

Tip To add a handful of friends to an existing list quickly, click the Add Multiple button that appears on the list page. In the dialog box that appears, scroll to browse through all your pals, clicking each Facebook friend you want to add to your list. When you finish, click Save List.

To delete friends from a list, follow the steps for adding a friend to an existing list; but in step 3, instead of typing a new name, mouse over the name of one of the folks already listed and then click the Edit Lists button that appears. Finally, on the drop-down list that appears, click the name of the list you want to delete the friend from (it has a checkmark next to it). Facebook removes the person from that list and deletes the checkmark.

Tip To delete a slew of friends from a list quickly: At the top left of any Facebook page, click the Account link and then click Edit Friends. On the left side of your Friends page, click the name of the list you want to thin. On the list page that appears, click the Add Multiple button. Then, in the dialog box that appears, scroll down to browse through all your pals, clicking each blue, checkmarked Facebook friend you want to delete from your list (the checkmark disappears after you click it to let you know that friend is off the list). When you finish, click the Save List button.

Deleting a Friend List

Maybe you created a Friend List and find you never use it. Or maybe the number of friends on one of your Friend Lists has dwindled to nothing. Whatever your reason, deleting a Friend List is easy:

1. **View the list you want to delete (page 64).**

2. **Head to the bottom of the list and click the Delete List link.** In the confirmation box that appears, click Confirm.

Breaking Up: Unfriending Friends

Breaking up is never easy, but sometimes you just gotta do it. Say one of your Facebook friends stabs you in the electronic back by posting inappropriate stuff on your Wall or spamming all your other friends, and you really have no choice but to cut him loose. To remove someone from your collection of Facebook friends:

1. **At the top right of any Facebook page, click the Account link and then click Edit Friends.**

2. **On the page that appears, click the Recently Interacted button and, from the drop-down list that appears, choose All Friends.**

3. **Scroll to the name of the person you want to "unfriend," and then click the X that appears to the right of his name.**

4. **In the confirmation box that appears, click "Remove from Friends."** You're friends no more.

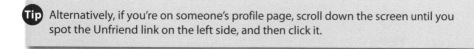

Tip Alternatively, if you're on someone's profile page, scroll down the screen until you spot the Unfriend link on the left side, and then click it.

Note Unlike quietly ignoring a friend request, unfriending someone sends a clear message. Because Facebook friendship is reciprocal, removing a friend means you disappear from your former friend's All Friends list—an unmistakable rebuff.

Chapter 4
Sending Messages to Friends

Just like your email program, Facebook lets you send private Messages to other Facebook members. "Great," you're probably thinking, "just what I need: yet another inbox to check." But before you skip to the next chapter, you might want to give these tools a chance.

First off, Facebook makes exchanging Messages dead simple—even easier than regular email. And then there are the slightly zany—but slightly addictive—ways to keep in touch with others that no email program can match. In an effort to mimic the different ways we interact with people in real life, Facebook lets you *poke* (give a virtual "Hey, how ya doin'?" wave to) friends and write on their virtual message boards for all their—and your—other friends to see, which can lead to the Facebook version of a group hug. Even if you're not persuaded by any of this, it's still worth understanding the messaging system since, soon enough, you'll no doubt get a Facebook Message from one of your friends.

Sending Messages

Lots of websites offer free web-based email, and Facebook is one of them—sort of. As a Facebook member, you can send private Messages to any other Facebook member (whether or not they're on your friend list) and to regular email addresses. But only other Facebook members can send *you* Facebook Messages. In other words, when you register for Facebook, you don't get a YourName@Facebook.com email account; instead, people have to sign up for Facebook and follow the steps below if they want to send a Message to your Facebook inbox.

 Note The way you send Messages on Facebook may change soon. Rumor has it that Facebook may start offering free email accounts.

Sending Messages to Friends

Most of the Messages you send, of course, will be to people you already know. Facebook gives you a simple set of tools that will look familiar if you've used email before. Here's what you do:

 Note If you like, you can send (and receive) Facebook Messages by texting on your cellphone. See Chapter 14 for details.

1. **At the top left of any Facebook screen, click the icon that looks like two speech bubbles, and then in the drop-down menu that appears, click the "Send a New Message" link**. Or, if you're on your Home page, click the Messages link on the left side of the screen and then click the New Message button on the right side of the page that appears. Either way, Facebook displays the New Message box.

2. **In the "To:" field of the New Message box, start typing your friend's name (if she's a Facebook member), email address (for non-Facebook members), or the name of a Friend List (page 63)**. As soon as you start typing, Facebook displays a list of your friends and Friend Lists. To select a name, click it or use the up and down arrow keys to select the name, and then hit Enter.

If you're sending a Message to a non-Facebook member, simply type in the person's full email address. You can add multiple recipients, if you like; just click the "To:" field again after you enter each one and then start typing again. (See page 72 for more on sending Messages to multiple people.)

Why would you want to use Facebook to send a Message to someone who's not a Facebook member? Two reasons: First, you're already in Facebook and don't have to waste time switching over to your email program (or can't, if you're using someone else's computer). Second, you want to lure this non-member friend into your Facebook social circle by giving her a taste of Facebook's coolness. When your friend clicks the Facebook-generated "Click to Reply" link in your email, she's whisked to a Facebook page she can use to preview Facebook messaging, as well as to get more info and sign up.

 Tip After you've added a recipient's name, you can delete it by clicking the X Facebook displays next to it, or by hitting the Delete key.

3. **Fill in the "Subject:" field and then type your Message.** If you want to pass along a link to a website (or to a photo or video on the Web), mouse down to the Attach section and click the photo, video, or link icon. When you finish, click Send.

4. **If a security box like the one on page 10 appears, type in the security words you see and then click Send.** Facebook sends your Message and stores a copy on your Sent Messages page, which you can view by heading to your Home page, clicking the Messages link on the left, and then clicking the Sent link that appears below it.

Sending Messages to People You're Not (Yet) Friends With

Facebook lets you send a Message to *any* member of the site, even if she's not on your friend list and doesn't belong to any of your networks.

 Note There's one exception to this rule: If a Facebook member *blocks* you (page 231), you can't contact him on the site—by sending him a Message, *poking* him, or in any other way.

To send a Message to a non-friend Facebook member:

1. **Head to the profile of the person you want to contact**.

2. **Click the Send Message button on the right side of the person's profile**. Up pops the New Message box shown on page 71. Simply type your Message and send it off as explained in the previous section.

Sending a Message to More Than One Person

Because Facebook was designed to help people communicate online just as they do offline, the site makes it easy to send a Message to an individual— but a little harder to send the same Message to dozens of people all at once. If you go too far down that path, the Facebook design team reasoned, you're talking spam. After all, how often do you whip out a bullhorn and address a real-life crowd of dozens?

Facebook decided to cap the number of people you can send a Message to at 20, so you can use the basic Message-sending instructions on page 70 and type in a combination of Facebook friends' names and email addresses to send your Message to up to 20 people. Another option is to create a Friend List (page 63) containing all the people you want to send the Message to. Then, in the New Message box, head to the "To:" field and type the name of the list. But know that if you try to send a Message to a Friend List that includes more than 20 people, Facebook will display a "Cannot add list" message and remind you of its 20-person limit.

 Note An exception to the no-spam rule is that Facebook lets you send the same Message to every member of an old *Group* (Chapter 6)—although even then, Facebook theoretically caps the number of recipients at 5,000. (The cap is theoretical because some Facebook members have had their accounts suspended for sending Messages to a lot fewer than 5,000 people.)

Receiving Messages

When someone sends you a Message via Facebook, two things happen:

- **You receive the Message in your Facebook inbox**. To alert you that you have a Message, Facebook displays a little red box above the Messages icon at the top left of any Facebook screen (it looks like two overlapping speech bubbles). To open your inbox, simply click the Messages icon. In the list that appears, you can either click the Message you want to read, or click the See All Messages link and then click any Message to see it in its entirety. (If you're on your Home page, you can also get to your Facebook inbox by clicking the Messages link on the left side of the screen.)

- **You receive the Message in your regular email program**. Facebook also sends the Message to your primary email address.

 Note Your primary email address is the one you used when you registered for the site (unless you've changed it since then). To change your primary email address, at the top of any Facebook screen, click Account and choose Account Settings; on the screen that appears, click Email.

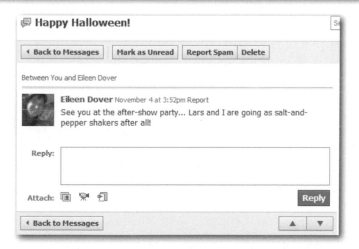

Tip If you spend a lot of time on the site and regularly check your Facebook inbox, you don't really need to have Facebook Messages sent to your regular email address, too. To make it so you only receive Facebook Messages in your Facebook inbox, head to the Email Notifications page (to get there, simply click the "Want to control which emails you receive from Facebook?" link at the bottom of any email Facebook sent to your regular email address) and turn off the checkbox next to "Sends you a message".

Viewing Your Facebook Inbox

It's easy to tell if you have a new Facebook Message even without opening your inbox. Just take a look at the blue menu bar at the top of any Facebook screen. If you see a red number right above the icon that looks like two little speech bubbles (it's the second icon to the right of the word "facebook"), you've got a new Message (or two, or more). Click that icon and a list of your most recent Messages appears. To see your full inbox, click the See All Messages link at the bottom of the list. Or, if you're on your Home page, simply click the Messages link on the left side of the screen to open your inbox.

Facebook puts a big blue dot in front of any Message you haven't read yet, and highlights the entire listing in light blue. Facebook automatically lists *all* your Messages, even ones you've already read. If you only want to see the ones you *haven't* read, click the word "Unread" above the list. Clicking a sender's name or picture shoots you directly to that person's profile, which is handy if you don't recognize him.

Reading and Responding to Messages

To read a Message in your inbox, click anywhere in its listing and Facebook displays the whole Message.

If the Message was sent just to you, you reply by simply typing your response in the Reply box, and then clicking the Reply button. To delete the Message without replying, click the Delete button near the top of your screen.

If the Message was sent to you and at least one other person, you have two options. You can reply to everyone by typing in the Reply box and then clicking the Reply All button. Or, if you just want to respond to the sender without bugging everyone else, click the tiny Reply link to the right of the sender's name. When you do, Facebook pops up a New Message box where you can type your response.

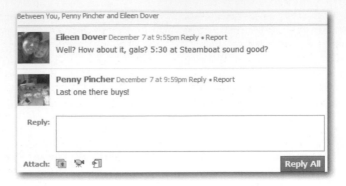

Chatting

Facebook's built-in chat feature lets you send messages to friends who are online when you are. Because chat messages—unlike regular Facebook Messages—pop up on your friends' screens immediately after you send them, they're handy for exchanging quick updates. ("Hey, we still meeting for lunch in 5 minutes?" "Yeah, I'm headed out the door now!")

To send a chat message:

1. **At the bottom right of any Facebook screen, click the** 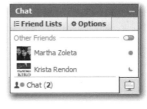 **button**. The number that appears in parentheses beside the word "Chat" tells you how many of your Facebook friends are currently logged into the site (and, therefore, how many folks you can potentially send chat messages to).

2. **In the Chat window that appears, click the name of the friend you want to chat with**. A green dot beside a person's name means he is logged in and active. A blue crescent moon means he's logged into Facebook but hasn't typed anything in a few minutes (and so may be out getting a cup of coffee).

3. **In the person-to-person window that appears, type your message and then hit Enter**. As soon as you do, your message appears on you friend's screen in a similar person-to-person chat window.

4. **Send additional chat messages, if you want, by repeating step 3**. When you're finished with your conversation, you can hide the chat window by clicking anywhere on the blue bar that runs across the top of it.

Note Because chat messages can pop up on your screen, they can be seriously annoy-ing. To keep super-chatty folks from being able to chat with you, put them on a list (page 63) named, say, SuperChatties. Then, in the Chat box (at the bottom of any Facebook screen, click Chat), click the Friend Lists tab and make sure the checkbox next to the SuperChatties list is turned on. Then when SuperChatties appears in the chat box, click the green-and-white Go Offline icon (it looks like a capsule on its side) to the right of the list's name. Doing so hides the fact that you're online (and, therefore, "chattable") from everyone on the SuperChatties list and changes the green-and-white Go Offline icon to a grey-and-white Go Online icon (which you can click when you're in the mood to field one of those long-winded conver-sations). If you don't feel like chatting with *anyone*, in the Chat window, click the Options tab and then click Go Offline.

When someone sends *you* a chat message, Facebook plays a sound and up pops the Chat window, where you see the sender's profile picture along with their message. To reply, simply type your message in the bottom of the window and hit Enter.

 Tip You can customize the Chat window so that it stays up all the time instead of pop-ping up, and so that it doesn't play a sound every time someone chats at you—both of which are useful if you expect to do a lot of chatting. In the Chat window (at the bottom of any Facebook screen, click Chat), click Options. Then turn off the checkbox next to "Play Sound for New Messages" and turn *on* the checkbox next to "Keep Online Friends Window Open".

Poking

Poking sounds a lot more provocative than it is. Giving someone a *poke* in Facebook is nothing more than the electronic equivalent of asking some-one, "Hey, what's up?" Pokes appear as a "You were poked by [name]" mes-sage on the recipient's Home page.

 Tip Poking—like sneaking up behind someone and tapping her shoulder—isn't really good for much beyond the yuk factor. Depending on you and your pals' tolerance for friendly nudging, poking either gets the award for Silliest Social Aid or Most Annoying Thing Ever. If you're in the latter camp, you'll find *Notifications* (page 88) similar but more useful.

Note Times have changed, and you can't just poke anyone on Facebook anymore; your pokee must be a friend, a friend-of-a-friend, or someone in one of your networks (Chapter 2). If you poke someone who doesn't normally have access to your profile, he'll be able to see the basic, work-, and education-related portions of your profile for a week post-poke. But letting a pokee see your profile is rarely a problem. After all, if you're that worried somebody might discover your passion for the Bay City Rollers, you shouldn't poke him in the first place.

To poke someone:

1. **Find the person you want to poke by viewing your friend list (page 65) or using Facebook's Search box (page 48).**

2. **On the person's profile page, head to the upper-right side and click the Poke button.**

3. **In the confirmation box that appears, click Poke.** You briefly see a "You have poked [name]" message, and the damage is done: Your poke message appears on the pokee's Home page, complete with a link she can use to poke you back.

Writing on Walls

One of the sections on every Facebook member's profile is a forum called the *Wall*. A Wall is a place for your Facebook pals to share interesting photos, videos, websites, and character insights. By default, the only people's Walls you can write on are your own and your friends'. But since Walls are part of profiles, anyone who can view your profile can see your Wall messages. You can think of Walls as a 21st-century version of the dry-erase message boards they used to have in dorm rooms: a relatively public, informal place to brag, tease, show solidarity, get attention, and occasionally impart useful information.

Writing on a Friend's Wall

Writing on someone's Wall is a more public way of expressing yourself than sending your friend a message, because all your friend's friends will see your Wall post (unless you remember to tell Facebook to keep it between you and your friend, as explained on page 219). Good candidates for Wall posts include thanks, congratulations, birthday greetings, and other tidbits your shared connections might find interesting or useful.

Tip To write on your *own* Wall, follow the steps below, but start at your own profile instead of a friend's. If you like, you can adjust who sees the stuff you put on your Wall by clicking the padlock icon next to the Share button on your profile).

To write on a friend's Wall:

1. **On your friend's profile page, make sure the Wall link on the left side of the page is selected**. At the top of the person's wall, you should see the word "Share" followed by a row of icons. If you don't see the Share label, you're out of luck: Your friend has restricted access to her Wall.

2. **Click the appropriate Share icon.** For example, if you simply want to write your pal a note, click the Post icon and then type your message in the text box that appears. If you want to upload a photo or video or add a link to a website, click the appropriate icon. Depending on which icon you click, Facebook displays additional fields and instructions for completing your attachment.

Tip You can skip typing in the *http://* part of the website's address if you like—Facebook automatically adds it for you.

3. **If you decided to share a link, choose which thumbnail you want to accompany your link**. Facebook pulls a description and a handful of thumbnails from the site for you to choose from. To check out the various thumbnails, click the arrow buttons. To skip the graphic, turn on the No Thumbnail checkbox.

4. **If you decided to share a link, type in a short message letting your friends know why you're sharing (if you like)**. When you mouse over the link's information, Facebook highlights it in bright yellow. Click any highlighted text to replace it with your own message.

5. **Click Share**. Your message appears on your friend's (and your) Wall.

Responding to a Wall Post

When someone writes on your Wall, you can have a chuckle and leave it at that, or you can respond in one of the following ways:

- **Write something on the poster's Wall**. Clicking the name or profile picture of the person who wrote on your Wall whisks you to the writer's profile, where you can click a Wall tab and leave your own post on *his* Wall.

- **Respond to the post on your own Wall**. Clicking the Comment link below the person's post skips the back-and-forth history and just lets you type in your response. Clicking Like adds your name—accompanied by a thumbs-up icon—to the post.

- **Delete the post**. You can delete any post from your own Wall, no matter who posted it. To do so, mouse over the post until an X appears on the right side of the post. Click the X, and then click Remove Post in the confirmation box.

Chapter 5
Exchanging Automatic Updates

Remember what keeping up with your friends *used to* require? Time-consuming emails ("Sorry it's been so long…"), potentially intrusive instant messages ("hello? u there?"), even the occasional in-person visit. Not anymore: Thanks to Facebook's easy-to-activate broadcast and subscription tools, staying in touch is easier than ever. *Subscriptions* and *Notifications*, for example, alert you when, say, your best friend uploads a new picture, your softball coach gets off work, or your study buddy posts his analysis of Macbeth. This chapter shows you how to sign up for and tweak these handy updates.

Types of Updates

Facebook offers four different ways you can get details about your friends' activities. Three (*News Feeds, Mini Feeds*, and *Notifications*) appear automatically—on your Home page, your profile, and in your notification inbox, respectively.

 Although the News Feed, Mini Feed, and Notifications are all hard-wired into your account, Facebook lets you customize the details you see in all three. Read on to learn how.

And, if you prefer to keep up with your pals without even logging into Facebook, you can sign up for customized web feeds called *subscriptions*. The following sections explain all these options.

 Facebook also offers one other kind of automatic update: It tells you when friends' birthdays are coming up. At the top of any Facebook screen, click the Account link and then click Account Settings. On the page that appears, click the Notifications tab and then, in the list that appears, scroll down to the Facebook section and turn on the checkbox next to "Has a birthday coming up (weekly email)" and you'll never again forget a friend's birthday, because the site sends you an email (no more than once a week) listing all your Facebook pals whose birthdays fall somewhere in the next week.

News Feeds: What Others Are Doing

Your *News Feed* is a constantly updated list of the things your Facebook friends are doing on the site: adding applications, writing on Walls, commenting on *Notes* (page 97) and photos, befriending each other, and so on.

Facebook calls the standard version of your News Feed "Top News." In this list, you see the actions Facebook thinks you'll find the most interesting, based on a lot of top-secret number-crunching, and it appears automatically on your Facebook Home page, front and center—you don't need to do anything special to see it. (Facebook calls each item in this Feed a *story*.)

If you're on your Home page and don't see your News Feed, head to the left of the page and double-check that the News Feed link is selected. If it's not, click it.

If you want to see more than just the Facebook-selected highlights, you can view a different version of your News Feed that displays an up-to-the-second list of *everything* your Facebook pals are up to (not just the stuff Facebook thinks you're interested in). To do so, head to your Home page and click the Most Recent link at the top of the page (if you don't see it, check the left side of your screen to make sure the News Feed link is selected). To switch back to just the highlights, click the Top News link.

Facebook doesn't let you do away with your News Feed or completely control what it shows, but you can customize it to show more (or less) of the activities—and the friends—you're interested in.

Customizing Your News Feed

In every social circle, you're bound to have some friends you're closer to than others. If you'd prefer to concentrate on just two or three friends' activities—or skip the who's-dating-who-this-week chatter and focus just on certain applications (Chapter 12) or Pages (page 174) you're interested in—you can customize your News Feed.

To see more (or less) of specific Facebook friends:

1. **On your Home page, click the Most Recent link**.

2. **Scroll down to the bottom of the screen and click the Edit Options link**.

3. **In the Edit Your News Feed Settings box that appears, use the "Show posts from" menu to control whose posts you see.** You can opt to see news about *all* your friends and Pages, or just the ones you interact with most.

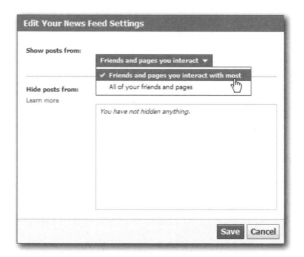

 News Feeds work both ways: Facebook keeps track of *your* actions on the site, too, and includes them in your friends' News Feeds. To learn how to prevent certain things you do from showing up on your friends' News Feeds, see page 222.

To hide a story that appears in your News Feed:

1. **On your Home page, make sure your News Feed is displayed**.

2. **Scroll down until you spot the story you want to hide**.

3. **Mouse over the story until an X appears in the upper-right corner of the story, and then click the X. In the drop-down list that appears, choose either "Hide this post" (to cut down on future stories involving this person) or "Hide all by [person/Page/application]" (to cut way down on future stories involving the same person, Page, or application).** If the story involves a Page (page 174), the drop-down list also includes an Unlike Page option, which you can click to remove stories about this Page from your News Feed *and* remove the Page from the Info section of your Profile (page 18).

 Clicking the "Mark as spam" option shoots an email to Facebook's technical staff letting them know that you believe this post was sent by someone you don't know and don't want to have anything to do with. Facebook takes spam accusations seriously: If enough folks mark a particular person, Page, or application (Chapter 12) as a spammer, the site may pull the plug on the offending party's account.

If you change your mind later and want to see stories about that person or application again, scroll to the bottom of your News Feed and click the Edit Options link. (Alternatively, at the top of your news feed, click the triangle next to Most Recent and then click Edit Options in the drop-down menu.) In the Edit Your News Feed Settings box that appears, in the "Hide posts from" section, find the person or item you want to see again, and then click the X that appears next to his (or its) name.

Mini Feeds: What You're Doing

Your News Feed keeps track of all the stuff your friends do on Facebook. Similarly, your *Mini Feed* (which appears on the Wall section of your profile interspersed with Wall posts) chronicles the stuff *you* do on Facebook—and that other folks do that directly affects you, like writing on your Wall or sending you a gift. Anyone who can see your profile can see your Mini Feed. (Unlike your News Feed, your Mini Feed isn't labeled; in other words, you don't see the words "Mini Feed" on your profile.)

Note Your Mini Feed doesn't contain *additional* information; it just aggregates the juicy bits displayed elsewhere on your profile and adds them to your *Wall* (page 78). So, what people can't see on your profile, they can't see on your Mini Feed. For example, if you RSVP to a secret event and your friend Ralph wasn't invited, he won't be able to find out he was snubbed by reading your Mini Feed.

Customizing Your Mini Feed

In addition to merging the Mini Feed with the Wall (they used to be separate), Facebook has reduced the amount of control you have over your Mini Feed. Fortunately, you can still customize your Mini Feed by removing individual *stories*. Stories that appear on your Mini Feed are accounts of specific things you've done on Facebook, such as commenting on someone's picture or updating your *status* (page 92).

To customize your Mini Feed:

1. **At the top right of any Facebook screen, click Profile.**

2. **On the left side of the page that appears, make sure the Wall link is selected (if it isn't, click to select it).**

3. **Scroll down the Wall section of your profile and read through the stories**.

4. **Delete any stories you don't want people to see**. To do so, mouse over the story so that an X appears to the right of it. Click the X (and, in the confirmation box that appears, click the Remove Post button) to delete that story from your Mini Feed.

Facebook Notifications

A *Notification* is a message telling you that something involving *you* happened on Facebook: Someone wrote on your Wall, for example, invited you to join a Group, or replied to something you said on a discussion board. You also get Notifications from the folks at Facebook from time to time.

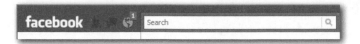

In the upper-left part of all Facebook screens, just to the right of the Facebook logo, are three little icons. The rightmost one, which looks like a tiny Earth, is the Notification icon. When you have a new Notification, Facebook displays a red box above the icon letting you know how many you have. Click the icon to see a list of your Notifications.

Notifications also appear in your regular email program's inbox, and, optionally, in your cellphone's inbox:

- **To see the email versions of your Notifications**, head to your email program and check your email just as you normally do.

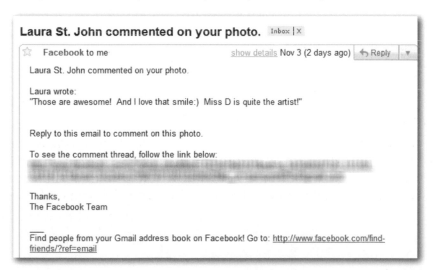

Subscribing to Notifications lets you see them as a *web feed* instead of in your email inbox. Page 92 tells you how.

- **To tell Facebook to send Notifications to your cellphone**, you first need to activate your cellphone on Facebook (see Chapter 14), and then tell Facebook which Notifications you want sent to your phone by following the instructions in the next section.

Choosing Which Notifications You Want to See and Where

Unless you tell it otherwise, Facebook assumes you want to be notified about a staggering amount of social minutiae. This means that, if you have more than two or three friends who actively use the site, your email inbox will overflow from all the Notifications you'll receive.

To specify what you want to be notified about—and what you *don't*—and how, follow these steps:

1. **At the top of any Facebook screen, click the Account link and then, in the drop-down list that appears, click Account Settings**.

2. **On the page that appears, click the Notifications tab**.

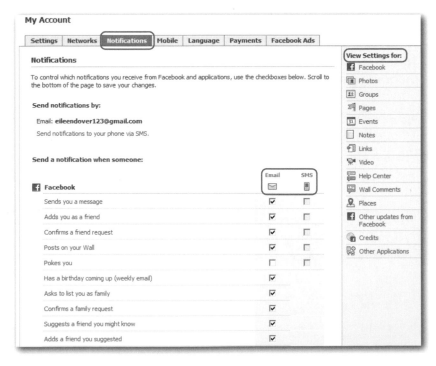

3. **Tell Facebook which activities you want to be notified about**:

— **To choose which activities you want learn about via email:** On the Notifications tab, head to the Email column, scroll down to see each activity, and turn off the checkbox next to any activity you don't want to get email about; alternatively, turn *on* the checkbox next to any activity you *do* want to get email about.

Tip Rather than scroll down the entire list of activities, you can click the links in the "View Settings for" list on the right side of the Notifications tab to hop directly to the type of activity you're interested in. For example, if you want to change which event-related Notifications you receive, click the Events link.

— **To choose which activities you want to learn about via cellphone:** After you've given Facebook your cellphone info (see page 237), you can tell the site to notify you of certain activities by sending Notifications directly to your phone. (You can't have as many types of Notifications sent to your cellphone as you can to your email program, but that's probably a good thing.) On the Notifications tab, head to the SMS column, scroll down to see each activity, and turn on the checkbox next to any activity you want sent to your phone (or turn *off* the checkbox next to any activity you *don't* want sent to your phone).

Note *SMS* stands for Short Message Service, which is the technology cellphones use to send and receive text messages.

4. **When you finish, scroll down to the bottom of the page and click Save Changes**.

Note Telling Facebook to send Notifications to your cellphone is also called *subscribing* to your Notifications. Facebook always displays friend requests and invitations to Groups and Events on your Home page, so the Notifications you get about these activities are redundant. Turn them off and you won't miss a thing (assuming you check your Home page from time to time).

Subscriptions

Technically, subscriptions are *web feeds*—those ubiquitous summary blurbs provided by web publishers like the *New York Times* and Reuters and known to geeks everywhere as RSS (which stands for Rich Site Summary or Really Simple Syndication depending on who you ask). Whatever you call them, think of a *subscription* as a continuously updated newsletter that's stored as a big chunk of data you can format and view however you like—as a basic, no-frills list of items on a web page, for example, or in a fancy online news reader.

 When you follow the steps on page 94, your subscription appears as a basic list on a web page. To see it in a different format, check out one of the many free news reader (a.k.a. *aggregator*) programs and services, such as Google Reader (*www.google.com/reader*) or Feed Demon (*www.feeddemon.com*). For an in-depth look at all things web feed, check out *http://oreilly.com/feeds*.

Subscriptions don't give you any info that you couldn't find by combing through Facebook, but they make that information easier to get to because it appears on a single web page that updates automatically. Plus, you don't have to log into Facebook to see it. And depending on which web browser you use, you can customize the way you see subscription info. For example, if you use Internet Explorer, you can sort your subscription info, specify how often you want to see updates, and even have your computer play a sound when the info gets updated.

You can sign up for one or more of the following:

- **A subscription that sends your friends' current statuses to your cellphone**. Typically a quick one-liner that your friends type in from time to time, such as "I'm leaving work" or "I'm at the library," a Facebook *status update* lets you know what your friends think is important enough to share. Signing up for a status subscription lets you track where your friends are and what they're doing or thinking at any given time without having to log into Facebook. Unlike the other subscription options, you can *only* subscribe to your friends' status updates by cellphone (see Chapter 14).

 To update *your* status, head to the top of your Wall or your News Feed (which is on your Home page), click the Status icon, and then click the "What's on your mind?" field. (As soon as you click the field, it appears empty.) Type whatever you want and, if you like, click one of the Attach icons to add a photo, video, or link (mouse over the icons to see which is which). When you're done, click the Share button, and Facebook updates your status so all your friends can see what you're up to.

 Note Facebook used to make it easy for you subscribe to the links your friends posted, but that's not the case anymore. Perhaps in anticipation of the recently announced Places application (page 245)—which gives you a way to keep up with the people, things, and places your friends think are cool—Facebook axed the official way of letting you subscribe to your friends' links. If you're determined to subscribe to your friends' links, however, you still can—for now, anyway. Here's what you do: First, in the Search field at the top of your Home page, type *links* and hit Enter. The My Friends' Links page that appears lets you choose whether to subscribe to links posted by everyone you're friends with or just a specific person. To subscribe to 'em all, click My Friends' Links in the "Subscribe to Links" section on the left side of the page. To pick a certain person, type his name where it says "Jump to Friend or Page," hit Enter, and then click "[Friend's name]'s Links" in the "Subscribe to Links" section. Finish up by following steps 4–6 on page 95.

- **A subscription that shows you the Notes your friends (or other Facebook members) are publishing, as they publish them**. (Flip to page 97 to learn about Notes.) Signing up for a Notes subscription helps ensure you don't miss a single exciting installment of your friends' blogs (er, Notes), even when you're not logged into Facebook. You can subscribe to Notes published by any Facebook member who chooses to syndicate her Notes (make them publicly available for subscription), even if you're not friends with her.

 Note Subscribing to your *own* Notes sounds weird (and a little narcissistic), but it's useful if you want to package your Notes for cutting and pasting to another blog service (see page 100).

- **A subscription that shows you all your Notifications**. Unless you tell it differently, Facebook assumes you want to see your Notifications (page 88) in your email inbox. But if you prefer, you can choose to have them sent to your cellphone—handy if you want to keep in touch with your Facebook pals without having to log into the site or comb through a mountain of emails.

Note Depending on what kind of cellphone and cellphone service you have, you may find that a Facebook application (such as "Facebook for iPhone" or "Facebook for BlackBerry") can be a handier—and cheaper—way to get cellphone access to Facebook than subscriptions. See page 236 for more info.

The following sections explain how to sign up for each of these subscriptions.

Subscribing to Friends' Status Updates

To stay up to the minute on your friends' doings, sign up for a status update subscription:

1. **Give Facebook your cellphone number and double-check that you can receive text messages from the site**. Facebook calls this *activating* your cellphone; Chapter 14 has the how-to.

2. **On any Facebook page, click Account, then Account Settings**.

3. **On the My Account page that appears, click the Mobile tab**.

4. **Scroll down to the "Whose status updates should go to my phone?" text field and start typing the name of the friend you want to track**. When Facebook displays a helpful list of friends, select the one you want.

5. **In the Mobile Subscriptions box that pops up, click Confirm**.

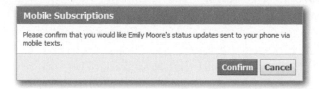

Tip If you change your mind and want to unsubscribe from someone's status updates, you can do so from your cellphone by responding to a status update text with the word "Unsubscribe."

Subscribing to People's Notes

Page 97 tells you all about *Notes* (Facebook's version of blogs). To subscribe to someone's Notes:

1. **Go to the person's profile (page 48), and then click the Notes link below the person's profile picture.** If you don't see a Notes link on a particular profile, it's either because the person hasn't written any Notes or because he adjusted his privacy settings to hide them (Chapter 13).

Tip To see which of your friends writes Notes: On the left side of your Home page, click the Notes link (you may have to click More to see it). Alternatively, type *notes* into the Search box at the top of any page and then hit Enter. Either way, Facebook displays all your pals' Notes.

2. **Head to the bottom of any Note and click the View Full Note link.**

3. **On the left side of the page that appears, look for the Subscribe header (you may have to scroll down to see it) and click the "Eileen Doe's Notes" link (or whatever the person's name is) below it.**

Note Exactly what you see on your screen during the next two steps depends on which web browser and feed reader you use. The examples shown should look familiar if you use Internet Explorer as your combined web-browser-and-feed-reader.

4. **On the page that appears, click "Subscribe to this feed" (or the similarly worded link that appears in your browser).**

5. **In the box that appears, choose the bookmark folder you want to put your subscription in**. The feed name Facebook suggests is perfectly workable, if a little boring, so you don't have to type in a new one (but you can if you want). Because you access subscriptions through your web browser, the folder you choose from the "Create in" drop-down list (or create using the "New folder" button) appears in your web browser's feeds list.

> **Tip** *Bookmarking* a web page makes it easy for you to return to that page again later. When you view your web browser's feeds list, you see the name of your subscription's bookmark folder; just click it to see the latest installment of your subscription. (How you view your feed list is different in every browser. To view it in Internet Explorer, for example, click the Favorites Center button—the tiny yellow star to the left of the main menu.)

6. **Click Subscribe**. Up pops a message telling you your subscription was successful. To see your subscription, you can either click the "View my feeds" link in the success message, or use your browser's menu to see all your feeds. If you use Internet Explorer, for example, click the Favorites Center icon (the little star on the left side of the menu) to view your feeds.

Tip If you're not thrilled with the way your web browser displays your subscriptions (a.k.a., feeds), you can use a free *news aggregator service*, such as FeedBucket (*www.feedbucket.com*) to display them instead. You need a feed's URL to view it using an aggregator. If you're using Internet Explorer as your web browser, click the Favorites icon (the little yellow star) and then the Feeds button. Then try right-clicking any feed in your feed listing, and then choosing Properties to see the feed's copy-and-paste-able URL that you need if you want to use a news aggregator service.

Creating Notes (Blogs)

Ever since the "blogosphere" replaced the more mundane "bunch o' personal websites," every site worth its salt offers free *blogs*—easy-to-use online journals where you can chronicle your hobbies, family or work life, or whatever you feel like writing about. Facebook offers free blogs, too—it just calls them *Notes* instead.

 Note There's a slight—but very important—difference between Notes and regular old blogs: Because Facebook integrates Notes with all the other stuff you do on the site (thanks to tagging, which is explained in a sec), Notes can actually document the complex social interactions between you and your friends (and your friends and *their* friends, and so on). It's scary, it's exciting, it's très 21st-century—and it's a marketer's dream come true.

You can either upload an existing blog (if you have one) into Facebook's Notes, or you can create your own Notes from scratch. And here's the cool part: You can *tag* your Notes. *Tagging* a Note means associating one or more of your Facebook friends' names with it. For example, say you write a Note describing the fishing trip you took with your pal Fred. You can tag the Note with Fred's name, making it easy for Fred—and his Facebook friends—to find your tale of the trip.

After you create a Note, Facebook lists the Note's subject line on your profile page (look for the Notes section) so other folks can find your Note and comment on it. At the same time, the site automatically sends Notifications to all the friends you tagged so they can check out what you said about them.

 Note By tweaking your Notes privacy settings (which you access by clicking the "Customize settings" link shown on page 147 and heading to the "Posts by Me" option), you can control who gets to know about, see, and comment on your Notes. Flip to page 147 for step-by-step details.

Typing Notes from Scratch

If you don't already have a blog, or you *do* have a blog but you don't want to cut and paste it into Facebook, you need to start fresh. To create your first blog installment on Facebook:

1. **On the left side of your Home page, click the Notes link**. If you don't see the Notes link, expand the menu by scrolling to the bottom of it and clicking the More link.

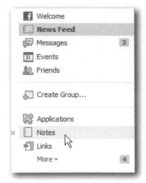

2. **On the Notes page that appears, click the "Write a Note" button**.

3. **On the "Write a Note" page, compose your Note.** Fill in the Title field with a subject line for your Note (think of it as a summary of your entry and shoot for provocative, concise, or both). In the Body field, type your Note.

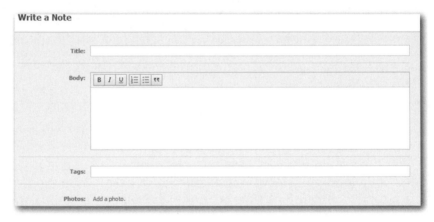

4. **If you want to, tag the Note**. Tagging is a way of associating the Note with a Facebook friend (or 10). For example, if your Note chronicles the office Christmas party, you might want to tag the officemates you mention. To tag your Note, click the "Tags" field and start typing; then choose one of the names Facebook helpfully displays.

 For a blow-by-blow on tagging, see page 166.

5. **If you like, add a photo or two**. To do so, click the "Add a photo" link, then click the Browse button that appears and, in the window that pops up, select the image file you want to add. Repeat this process to add more photos.

6. **If you want to, restrict who will get to see your Note**. Facebook assumes you want *everyone* to see your Note. If that isn't the case, click the drop-down list that appears next to the Privacy label and choose "Friends Only," "Friends of Friends," or one of the other options.

7. **Click the Preview button to give your note a quick once-over**. Double-check what you've written and the formatting, which can get a little funky (especially if you added photos). If you see something you don't like, click the Edit button to change your Note. Then repeat the preview-edit cycle until you're happy with the result. If you don't have time to perfect your Note now, click the Save Draft button; you can then come back later and finalize your Note using the process explained in the following Tip.

 Tip If you accidentally surf away from the Notes page before you have a chance to finish editing your Note, Facebook's got your back: It saves what you've got so far. To find and finish editing (or, if you prefer, to delete) your note-in-progress: On the left side of your Home page, click Notes (you may have to click the More link to see it), and then click the My Drafts link that appears.

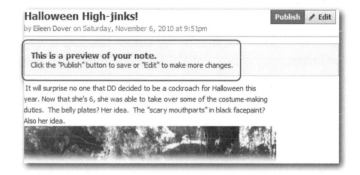

Note Facebook uses *HTML* (hypertext markup language) to format Notes. If you know HTML, use it: Type HTML tags directly into the Body field along with your text. To learn more about HTML, check out *Creating a Web Site: The Missing Manual, Second Edition*.

8. **Click the Publish button**. Facebook lists your new Note in the Notes section (or tab; see page 97) of your profile, on your Wall for all the world (technically, all the folks you specified in step 5) to see and comment on, and sends Notifications to the folks you tagged (if any).

Tip After you publish your Note, you can share it with people who aren't yet on Facebook. To do so: Go to the Notes page (see step 1 above) and then, on the left side of your screen, click My Notes. Then click the title of the Note you want to share and, on the page that appears, click the Share button. In the "Post to Profile" box that appears, click the "Send as a Message instead" link; then, in the "To:" field of "Send as a Message" box, type the email address of the person you want to share your Note with and then click Send Message.

Importing Notes from an Existing Blog

If you've already got a blog on some other site (such as *www.typepad.com* or *www.blogger.com*), you can tell Facebook to duplicate your blog entries as Facebook Notes. That way, the people on Facebook can read your musings without your having to type every blog entry twice.

 Note You can't use Facebook to *edit* the Notes you import from a blogging site. Instead, you have to edit your Notes using the other blogging service's website, just as you do now. Think of Facebook's version as merely a reprint.

To import blog entries from an existing blog into Facebook:

1. **In the Search field at the top of any Facebook page, type *notes* and then hit Enter**.

2. **On the left side of the Friends' Notes page that appears, click the "Edit import settings" link (you may have to scroll down to see it)**.

3. **On the "Import a Blog" page, head to the Web URL field and type in your blog's web address (like *http://YourNameHere.blogspot.com*, for example)**. Turn on the "By entering a URL…" checkbox to reassure Facebook that the blog you're importing is yours (it needs to be; adding anything to your Facebook account that you haven't personally created or bought rights to distribute spells copyright infringement), and then click the Start Importing button.

4. **On the confirmation page that appears, click Confirm**. Facebook adds the imported blog entries to your from-scratch Notes.

Viewing and Changing Your Notes

Facebook makes it easy to see all the Notes you've written, and change or delete them one at a time. To see and edit your Notes:

 If you import Notes, you can't edit them in Facebook. You can, however, see and delete them by following the steps below.

1. **On the left side of your Home page, click the Notes link (you may have to click More to see it).**

2. **On the left side of the Notes page that appears, click the My Notes link (it's just below the Notes link you clicked in step 1).**

3. **Find the Note you want to edit or delete and click its title.**

4. **On the page that appears, click either the Edit button or the Delete link.**

Restricting Access to Your Notes

Unless you tell Facebook otherwise, *all* your Facebook friends and fellow network members can see, subscribe to, and comment on the Notes you write. But you can customize access to your Notes either before you publish them (page 99) or after the fact so that:

- All Facebook members can see your Notes.
- Only the people in certain networks (such as your work network or school network) and friends of the folks *you're* friends with can see them.
- Only your friends and the people in your networks can see them.
- Only your friends and your friends' friends can see them.
- Only your friends can see them.
- No one can see them (think personal online journal).
- Only specific friends can see (or *not* see) them.
- Only certain people can comment on them (for example, friends of friends, only friends, or only the people you list).

 Tip For the scoop on subscriptions, see page 92.

To modify who can access your Notes after you've created them:

1. **On the left side of your Home page, click the Notes link (you may have to click More to see it).**

2. **On the left side of the Notes page that appears, click the My Notes link (it's just below the Notes link you clicked in step 1) and then click the title of the Note you're interested in.**

3. **On the screen that appears, click the Edit button.**

4. **Scroll down the screen that appears and click the drop-down box next to "Privacy".** From the list, choose the set of folks you want to be able to see the Note. (Clicking Customize lets you get seriously picky about who you want—and don't want—to see your Notes.)

5. **When you're done, click the Save button.**

If you know you're always going to want the same bunch of people to see every Note you write—and you plan on writing a lot—you can save time by telling Facebook your preference once and letting the site apply that setting to each Note. (You can always tweak your preference later, on a per-Note basis.) Simply head to the top of any Facebook page and click the Account link, and then click Privacy Settings. Near the bottom of the page that appears, click the tiny "Customize settings" link. Finally, scroll down and click the "Posts by Me" drop-down list and then select the group of folks you want to let see your Notes.

To change who can add public comments to your Notes:

1. **At the top of any Facebook screen, click the Account link and, in the drop-down list that appears, click Privacy Settings**.

2. **Near the bottom of the Privacy Settings page that appears, click the "Customize settings" link.**

3. **On the page that appears, scroll down to the "Things others share" section, click the "Can comment on posts" drop-down box, and then make your selection**.

Adding Comments to Notes

Every time Facebook displays a Note that you (or anyone else) has created, it also displays a link people can use to comment publicly on that Note, either by typing a message or by leaving a virtual thumbs-up.

Comments give the people who read your Notes an easy way to stroke your ego, give you advice, or post helpful resources. And because the comments people leave appear one after the other, right after the text of your Note, they're easy to see and to change. On a Note's page, you can:

- **Add a comment to someone else's Note**. However you stumble across someone's Note—by viewing your friends' Notes (on the left side of your Home page, click the Notes link) or by going to the Notes section of a fellow network member's profile—the way you add a comment is the same: Simply click the Comment link or the "Write a comment" field that appears at the bottom of the Note, type your piece, and then click the Comment button that appears as soon as you start typing. (If you don't see this button, it's because the note writer told Facebook to remove it—see page 103.)

 Note Unless you tell it otherwise, Facebook automatically notifies you when someone comments on one of your Notes. (Page 222 tells you how to change this behavior.)

- **View the comments other people have added to your Note**. On the left side of your Home page, click Notes (you may need to click the More link first) and then click the My Notes link. Then click the "View all [number] comments" link below your Note to see all the comments people have made.

- **Delete a comment someone has added to your Note**. Perhaps someone added an offensive comment, or just one you'd prefer your friends not to see. To get rid of it, mouse over the comment and then click the X that appears on the right side of it; then, in the confirmation box that appears, click Delete.

 Tip If someone leaves an inappropriate comment—and overzealous marketing people, among others, have been known to do just that—you've got a couple options beyond simply deleting it: You can block that person from seeing your Notes or report him to Facebook (page 232).

Tagging Notes

Tagging a Note links that Note to one or more of your friends, whether or not the person is actually mentioned in the body of the Note. It's a win-win situation: Your friends get warm fuzzies from being tagged (everybody likes to feel important), you get more folks reading your Notes, and the companies that advertise on Facebook get a more complete picture of your social network.

You can tag a Note while you're creating it—as explained on page 98—or after you've published it. To do so:

1. **On the left side of your Home page, click the Notes link (you may have to click More to see it).**

2. **On the left side of the Notes page that appears, click My Notes.**

3. **Find the Note you want to tag and click its title.**

4. **On the screen that appears, click the Edit button to the right of the Note's title.**

5. **In the "Tags" field, start typing the name of the friend you want to tag.** Facebook pops up names as you type; click to select one. You can tag as many of your friends as you like.

6. **Scroll down to the bottom of the page and click the Save button.**

Finding Mentions of Yourself in People's Notes

Just as you can tag Notes with your friends' names, they can tag their Notes with yours. To see a list of all your friends' Notes that mention you:

1. **On the left side of your Home page, click the Notes link (you may have to click More to see it).**

2. **On the left side of the Notes page that appears, click the Notes About Me link.** All the Notes your friends have tagged with your name appear.

 Note *You* would never write a Note describing a scene of wild debauchery and then tag a squeaky-clean, trying-to-land-an-important-job friend (thus ruining any chance she has of passing her pre-interview background check), but some people would. Fortunately, Facebook lets you delete tags, even if someone else added them. On the Notes About Me page, scroll down to the Note you want to disassociate yourself from, click the Note's title, and—under the "Tagged" heading that appears on the left side of the page—click the "Remove my tag" link.

Chapter 6
Participating in Groups

Back in the day, Facebook Groups were collections of people who shared any interest, from the serious (such as membership in the same study group or work team) to the downright silly (like the desire to set a new record for the largest Facebook Group). Recently, however, Facebook redesigned its Groups feature to behave closer to the way small- to medium-sized real-world groups work. (Let's face it: Membership in one of those giant 500,000-member Groups of old wasn't particularly useful, other than to signal your approval of the group's stated purpose—and now you can express that approval by clicking the Like buttons described on page 175.)

 Tip If you find yourself missing those mega-Groups of yore, you have another option: Pages (see page 174).

The new-and-improved Groups are super useful for doing the kinds of things most people want to do in regular, real-life group situations. For example, Group members can post pictures that are only visible to other Group members; send an email to all the other Group members; chat online with other Group members in real time; and even add their two cents to a single, shared document.

This chapter shows you how to find, join, and participate in Groups—and how to start your own.

Facebook didn't remove the old Groups; they're still out there for you to find and enjoy (page 117). Just keep in mind that the old Groups don't work the same way as the new ones.

What's a Group?

There are two kinds of Groups on Facebook:

- **New Groups.** A new Group is a handful (or more) of Facebook friends who share a reason for keeping in regular touch with each other. Examples of good Group candidates include families who want to share photos of the kids; study buddies who want to exchange stuff they've found on the Web; former classmates planning a reunion; and support groups who want to share tips, advice, and encouragement. Groups don't have to be 100% virtual, either: Lots of groups that meet in person use Facebook Groups to keep in touch between meetings.

 Group-related *Events* make it super easy for Facebook members to organize face-to-face meetings; see Chapter 7 for details.

Whoever starts a Group gets to decide who the original members are. Once you're a member of a Group, you get to do things like post messages and pictures on the Group's bulletin board, add more Group members, create and attend Group-related events, and chat in real-time with fellow Group members.

 It may seem weird that someone else can decide, willy-nilly, that you're in a Group. (It's not so weird if you think of the new Groups as a souped-up version of the seldom-used Friend Lists described on page 63.) But just because someone taps you for membership in a Group doesn't mean you have to participate. You can turn off Group Notifications (page 111) so that you don't have to hear about any of the Group's goings-on, or you can leave the Group altogether (page 112).

- **Old Groups.** Old Groups are left over from the days when Groups looked and acted more like Facebook Pages. Members of old Groups can't chat together, send email to the entire group, or jot notes on the same scratch pad document the way members of new Groups can. If you're a member of an old Group, you can write to the Group's Wall, but that's about it.

As this book goes to press, new Groups are still pretty new, and telling the difference between them and old Groups can be tricky. (It doesn't help that Facebook simply calls both versions "Groups".) Fortunately, this chapter explains both kinds and tells you how to create your own Group.

 Note Technically, Groups is a Facebook *application* (page 197), so it's not a built-in part of Facebook. Chances are you'll never care about this distinction *unless* you decide to replace Groups with another application (see Chapter 12).

Joining a New Group

You don't so much join new Groups as agree to participate in them. That's because, unlike old Groups, you can't sign up for new Groups—you just have to wait until someone adds you to a new Group.

After someone adds you to a new Group, two things happen:

- **You receive a notification in your email program.** The email lets you know who added you and what the name of the new Group is. It also contains a link you can use to tell Facebook how often you want to be notified of the Group's activities (page 111).

- **The name of the Group appears on the left side of your Home page**.

 Tip Maybe your Home page is already clogged to the gills with Groups, and you don't want to see yet another one that you're not even sure you want to participate in yet. To remove the new Group from your Home page, click its name; then, on the Group page that appears, click Edit Settings. Turn off the checkbox next to "Show this group in home navigation" and then click Save Settings.

Participating in New Groups

What you can do in a new Group depends on whether you're an administrator or a regular member. (The person who creates a new Group is automatically an administrator of that Group. An administrator can designate other administrators—or not—at her discretion.) For example, administrators can change the way a Group works by changing its privacy settings and collective email address, and kick out unwanted members. Regular members can't do any of those things, but they can send emails to all the other members and post on the Group's page, and decide what kind of Group-related notifications they want Facebook to send them. The following sections have the details.

If You're a Group Member

As a regular member, you can:

- **Add messages, photos, videos, and links to the Group's page**. To do so: On your Home page, click the name of the Group. (You may have to click See All first.) Then, in the Group page that appears, click one of the Share options: Post (to post a message), Link, Photo, or Video.

- **Chat in real-time with other Group members.** To confer with all the Group members who haven't disabled Group chat (page 77) and who are currently online (and, thus, "chattable"): On your Home page, click the name of the Group; then, on the right side of the Group's page, click "Chat with Group." In the Group Chat box that pops up, type your message and hit Enter. When you finish chatting, click the X in the box's lower right.

- **Create (or edit) a shared document.** You and your fellow Group members can make changes to the same documents—think virtual whiteboard—to create lists, update schedules, or hammer out ideas. To create a shared document: On your Home page, click the name of the Group. Then, in the Share section of the Group's page, click the Doc link. After you make your additions, click Save.

  To edit a shared document that a fellow Group member created: On the Group's page, scroll down to the document you want to edit and click the View Doc link. On the doc's page that appears, click the Edit link.

 Note Your Group can share more than one document.

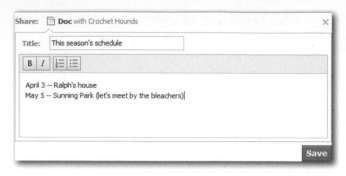

- **Tell Facebook which Group-related activities you want to be notified about and whether you want the Group to appear on your Home page.** For example, you might want to know when fellow Group members are chatting; if, on the other hand, you love 'em but know they're a chat-happy bunch, you might emphatically *not* want to know every time they engage in yet another chat fest. To set your preferences, in the upper-right part of the Group's page, click the Edit Settings button. In the "Edit Settings for [Group name]" dialog box that appears, tweak the various settings to your liking ("in home navigation" means "on your Home page"). If you'd like even more fine-grained control over when Facebook sends you notifications, click the "edit your notifications settings" link. On the Notifications page that appears, click to turn off the appropriate checkboxes and then click Save Settings.

> **Tip** If you set "Show this group in home navigation" to Never, the Group's name won't show up on your Home page, but you can see a list of all your Groups by clicking the See All link that appears under the Create Group link on the left side of your Home page.

- **Add friends to the Group.** On the right side of the Group's page, click the "Add Friends to Group" link. In the dialog box that appears, type your buddy's name and then click Add.

- **Post a message to the Group's page from your email program.** If one of your Group administrators set up a Group email address (page 115), that address appears on the Group's page, just below the Group's name. Sending an email from your email program to that address posts the message on the Group's page for all the Group's members to see. Depending on how each member has set up his Notifications (see page 111), he receives an email when someone posts to the Group's page.

- **Create a Group-related Event**. A *Group-related Event* is an *Event* (Chapter 7) that shows up on the Group's page. When you set up this kind of Event, Facebook automatically sends an invitation to all the Group's members. To create such an Event: Near the top of the Group's page, click the Event link, then the Add Details link that appears; then follow the steps on page 125.

- **Leave the Group**. Just because someone stuck you in a Group doesn't mean you have to stay. To opt out: On the right side of the Group's page, click the Leave Group link, and then click the Leave Group button in the confirmation box that appears. Leaving a Group means you no longer see the Group listed on your Home or Groups page, and you no longer receive notifications about Group activities.

If You're a Group Administrator

If you create a new Group (which you'll learn how to do in the next section), you're automatically the administrator. The other way to become a Group admin is to ask an existing Group administrator to make you one.

Group admins can do everything members can do, plus:

- **Create a Group email address.** Step 5 on page 115 explains how.

- **Change the way the Group works.** To change the Group's name, privacy settings, email address, or profile picture: On the Group's page, click the Edit Group button. On the Basic Information page that appears, tweak the Group's name or privacy settings (explained in the next section). When you finish, click Save Changes. To change or add a Group's profile picture, head to the left side of the Basic Information page and click Profile Picture.

- **Delete members.** On the Group's page, click the Edit Group button; then, on the left side of the page that appears, click the Members link. Scroll through the members and click the X next to the member you want to kick out of the Group; in the confirmation box that appears, click Confirm. (If you want to make sure that the member can *never* rejoin the Group, turn on the Ban Permanently box before you click Confirm.)

- **Grant members administrator status.** Because an administrator has the power to boot members out of the Group, she typically sets the tone of exchanges between members. If yours is a particularly active or demanding Group, tapping a fellow member or two as co-admins may give you much-needed backup when it comes to reining in Group member behavior. To give another Group member administrator status: On the Group's page, click the Edit Group button. Then, on the left side of the page that appears, click Members. Finally, click the Make Admin link next to the member you want to anoint and then, in the confirmation box that appears, click Make Admin again.

Creating a New Group

Creating your own Group makes it easier to keep in touch with out-of-town family, study buddies, team members, or any other collection of real-world folks. Because you can easily post baby pictures, assignments, and other stuff for Group members only, creating a Group also makes it a bit simpler to keep private matters private.

To start your own Group:

1. **On the left side of your Home page, click the Create Group link (you may have to click the More link first).**

2. **Fill out the Create Group box**. The fields are short and sweet: All you need to do is type in a name for your Group, then click the Members field and begin typing the names of the friends you want to be in the Group (as you type, Facebook pops up a helpful list for you to choose from).

You can also adjust the Privacy setting, if you like. Facebook assumes you want to create a Closed Group, which means that the Group's activities are private but that other Facebook members can see who's in the Group. If these are bad assumptions, click the Privacy drop-down menu and choose Open (meaning the Group's membership *and* activities can be seen by any Facebook member with access to at least one Group member's profile) or Secret (meaning neither the Group's membership nor activities is visible to anyone who's not a member of the Group). When you finish, click Create.

Tip Once you create (or are added to) a Group, Facebook displays the Group's name on the left side of your Home page along with an icon (unless you tell it not to, as explained on page 111). Fortunately, you're not stuck with the bland, two-headed icon Facebook automatically assigns to all Groups. If you're a Group admin, you can choose a different icon for your group—anything from a briefcase (suitable for a group of work buddies) to a filmstrip (perfect for a group of art-film buffs). To select a new icon for your Group, in the Create Group box, click the drop-down list just to the left of the Group Name field and then click the icon you want to use instead. (If you want to change the icon *after* you create the Group, head to the Group's page, click the Edit Group button, and then click the icon drop-down list.)

3. **In the confirmation box that appears, click Okay**. Facebook displays the new Group's page. From there, you can add a Group profile picture (explained next), set up a Group email (see step 5), change your privacy setting (page 117), add more friends to the Group (page 116), or chat with Group members (page 76).

4. **Upload a photo, if you like**. To do so, on the Group's page, click the Edit Group button. Then, on the Basic Information page that appears, click the "Add a profile picture" link. (Alternatively, you can click the Profile Picture link that appears below the thumbnail placeholder image.) A box appears so you can browse to find an image file on your computer that you want to associate with your Group, like a photo, drawing, or logo. After you finish, this picture appears on your—and other Group members'—Group page.

5. **Optionally, set up a Group email address.** Creating a Group address lets any member of your Group shoot a message from his email program to all the other members of the Group via the Group's page. To set up a Group email address: On the Group's page, click the Edit Group button. Then, on the Basic Information page, click the Set Up Group Email button and, in the box that appears, type in the first half of an email address (the part before the @ symbol; your Group's name is a good choice) and then click Create Email. (If the email address you want is taken, Facebook displays the message "[desired address] is not available." Keep trying until you pick one that's available.) Now, when a Group member sends an email to the address you just created, the text of the email appears on the Group's page. (The Group's email address appears on the Group's page right below the Group's name.)

6. **Describe your Group to give members an incentive to participate**. This step is also optional, but it's a good idea. Typing a one-liner that describes the purpose of your Group (such as "to plan our weekly get-together" or "to make sure we all pass Freshman Comp" sets the tone and helps members decide whether they want to become involved—or beat a hasty retreat. On the Group's page, click the Edit Group button. Then, on the Basic Information page that appears, type a line or two in the Description field. (The description you write appears in the "you've been added to the group" email that Facebook sends new Group members.) When you're done, click Save Changes.

 Note After you create a Group, you may want to tweak your Notification settings (see page 111) to tell Facebook how often you want to be alerted about Group activities.

Adding Friends to a New Group

You can add Group members while you're creating a new Group (page 113) or after the fact.

 Note You don't have to be a Group administrator to add friends to a Group.

To add friends to a Group:

1. **Head to the Group's page**.

2. **On the right side of the page that appears, click the "Add friends to Group" link**.

3. **In the "Add Friends to Group" box that appears, begin typing the name of a friend.** When Facebook helpfully pops up the profile picture of the friend you want to add, click it. You can repeat the type-and-click process to list additional friends, if you like. When you're finished, click Add.

Changing a New Group's Privacy Setting

You may have tweaked your Group's Privacy setting when you created the Group (page 113). If not, no problem—you can adjust that setting any time:

1. **Head to the Group's page and click the Edit Group button.**

2. **Click the Privacy drop-down list and choose a new setting (your options are explained in step 2 on page 114).**

3. **After you make your selection, click Save Changes.**

Deleting a New Group You Started

Sometimes you goof or change your mind. If you started a Group but a couple minutes later decide it wasn't such a great idea, you can delete it. Here's how:

1. **On the right side of the Group's page, click the Leave Group link.** If you're the one-and-only member of a Group, leaving the Group tells Facebook to delete it. If you're *not* the lone member, leaving the Group means the Group still exists—just without you in it.

2. **In the confirmation box that appears, click Remove (or Leave Group, as the case may be).**

 Note You can only delete a Group that you started. What's more, as soon as somebody else joins your Group, Facebook yanks your ability to delete it. What you *can* do at that point is step down as administrator. (When you do, Facebook is *supposed* to offer the gig to the remaining members of the Group. Currently, however, giving up your administrator gig simply leaves the Group without a leader. To avoid this, appoint another member administrator before you step down: On the Group page, click Edit Group, then Members. Then click the Make Admin link next to the member you want to pass the baton to.)

Finding, Joining, and Participating in Old Groups

There are still plenty of old Groups on Facebook—social-, craft-, business-, and sports-related Groups, as well as silly ones like "If A Million People Join This Group I will Change My Middle Name to Facebook." You can find and join these Groups, you just can't create new ones.

 Note Old Groups differ from new Groups in a few very important ways. In an old Group, only the head honcho (administrator) can email all the Group's members; in a new Group, any member can contact all the others with a single email. Old Groups also don't make it easy for Group members to chat with each other or let them contribute to a shared document; new Groups do. You can think of old Groups as being similar to Facebook Pages (page 174): good primarily for publicly signaling your approval of a certain topic or activity.

Searching for Old Groups

To find old Groups:

1. **In the Search box at the top of any Facebook screen, type your search word(s), and then click the magnifying glass icon**.

2. **On the left side of the search results page that appears, click the Groups link**.

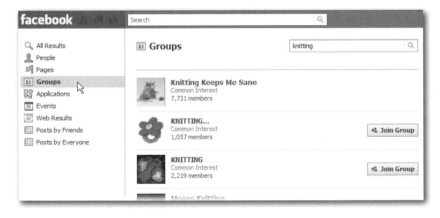

3. **If you spot a listing you're interested in, click either the Group's name or its picture**. Facebook displays the old Group's profile page so you can learn more.

Note Because Facebook recently pulled the ability to see which Groups—if any—your friends have joined, using the Search box now is the only way to ferret out old Groups.

Joining an Old Group

Facebook lets you join up to 200 Groups total (a combination of old and new ones), so if you like, you can go wild and join one for each of your diverse interests, and a few just for fun.

To join an old Group:

1. **Go to either the search listing (page 118) or the profile page of the Group you want to join**.

2. **Click the Join Group or Join button, respectively**.

3. **In the confirmation box that appears, click Join**. If the Group is *open*, that's it—you're in. If the Group is invitation only, Facebook sends your request to the Group's administrator, and you have to wait for approval.

After you've joined a Group, click the See All link on the left side of your Home page and you'll see your new Group listed on the Groups page.

Chapter 7
Facebook and the Real World: In-Person Events

Connecting with online pals in the real world is becoming more and more popular. Facebook's Event listings help you find out what's going on in your own backyard—everything from birthday parties and gallery openings to study sessions and protest marches. And because RSVPing to Events lets your Facebook friends see that you're planning to attend, a tiny get-together can quickly burgeon ("Well, hey, if Bob and Muffy are going, then *I'm* going!"). This chapter shows you how to find out what Events are happening in your area, who's attending, and how to set up your own Events.

Types of Events

Meeting people face-to-face raises privacy issues that don't exist online. As creepy as someone might be online (leaving weird or threatening notes on your Wall, poking you a hundred times a day, or becoming a fan of every Page you become a fan of), the worst risks you take are annoyance, embarrassment, and the possible filching of some personal data, all of which Chapter 13 helps you prevent. In person, though, that same creepiness could conceivably translate into actual bodily harm. So be *extremely* careful if you arrange a real-life meeting with someone (or a group of people) you met on Facebook.

To help deal with the privacy issues and safety concerns raised by in-person Events, Facebook offers these Event types:

- **Public Events**. Any Facebook member can read about this kind of Event on the Event's profile page and add himself to the guest list. Public Events are great for festivals, concerts, and other get-togethers held in public venues. You know an Event is public by the RSVP link on its search listing description (page 123), and by the "Public Event" message that appears just below the name of the Event at the top of the Event's profile page.

- **Private Events**. Only people who receive an invitation (either via Facebook notification or email) can tell that these Events exist. Go with this kind of Event when you're planning a business meeting, private party, or intergalactic invasion.

 Note: The *event administrator*—the person who dreams up the Event, adds it to Facebook, and manages the guest list—gets to decide which type it is.

Finding Public Events

Facebook gives you two ways to find Events you might want to attend:

- **Search for Events**. You can find Events using the Search box at the top of any Facebook page.
- **Check out the Events your friends plan to attend**. There's a good chance you'll be interested in the activities your friends enjoy.

Searching for Events by Name or Subject

If you know the name or subject of the Event you're looking for—or at least a word or two of the name or subject—the easiest way to find it is to search for it directly.

 Tip: It probably goes without saying, but for you to be able to look up a karate-related Event, the Event's creator has to put the word "karate" in the Event's name or somewhere in its description. (Page 125 explains how to create your own Events.)

To do so:

1. **At the top of any Facebook screen, click the Search field, type the name of an event or words you want to search for (such as "Pep"), and then click the magnifying glass icon**.

2. **On the left side of the search results page that appears, click the Events link to see the Events Facebook found**.

3. **Click the name of an Event to see its profile page**. The page that appears describes the Event in detail and lists confirmed and possible attendees (scroll down to see all the particulars).

 Note Facebook doesn't distinguish between global and regional Events anymore: *Every Facebook Event is global* (meaning anyone can see it, no matter what part of the world they live in). Facebook also doesn't let you sort through Events based on when they're being held or what kind they are (school-related, sports-related, or whatever). So if you're trying to find only those Events that will be held in your neck of the woods or only ones designated as parties, alas—there's no easy way to do that.

Seeing Your Friends' Events

Checking out the Events your friends are going to can be illuminating. ("Ralph's into cross-stitch? No *way!*") It might also turn up Events that *you're* interested in attending. Here's how: On the left side of your Home page, click the Events link. Then, on the left side of the Events page that appears, click the Friends' Events link and peruse the listings.

RSVPing to an Event

Sure, you *could* show up at an event without RSVPing first, but that would be rude! It would also mean that you'd miss out on the social networking benefits Facebook offers, because as soon as you RSVP, all your friends can see where you're headed—which may encourage them to join in the fun.

Depending on how the Event's administrator set things up (page 127), other folks in the network associated with the Event may be able to see that you're planning to attend.

There are two ways to RSVP to an Event:

- **If you received an invitation**, simply respond to it by following the instructions in the email or Facebook Notification. You can be invited to any kind of Event (public or private—see page 127), but the *only* way to RSVP to a private Event is by responding to an invitation, since you wouldn't even know about the Event if you hadn't been invited.

 To see your Event invitations on Facebook, simply check the right side of your Home page, under the Events heading. Alternatively, click the Events link on the left side of your Home page.

- **If you weren't explicitly invited**, head either to the Event's listing (page 123) and click the RSVP button, or to its profile page (page 123). In either case, click either "I'm Attending" or "Maybe" and you're in. Facebook updates the Event's profile page to show that you're a confirmed guest, and gives you new options you can use to change your response (to "Maybe" if your plans change, for example) or to invite other people. Facebook also adds the Event to the list on your Events page (which you can see by heading to the left side of your Home page and clicking the Events link).

 Whether or not you can invite other people depends on how the Event's administrator set the Event up. If, on the "Create an Event" page, the administrator turned off the "Anyone can view and RSVP (public event)" and turned on the "Guests can invite Friends" checkbox that magically appeared, you *can* invite your friends to join you at the get-together; otherwise, you can't.

After you RSVP, you can post text, photos, video clips, or links to the Event's profile page. To do so: On the left side of your Home page, click the Event link, then click the name of the Event. Then head to the "Write something" field and either type in some text or click the Link, Photo, or Video link. When you finish, click the Share button.

Creating Your Own Events

Whether you want to host a product launch party, start a study group at the local coffee shop, or have a community meeting, it's easy to set up your own Events on Facebook.

 Note If an Event is closely tied to a Facebook Group you created or that you've been made administrator of—you want to set up a face-to-face meeting of your book club, for example—you'll want to head to your Group's profile page and then click the Event link near the top of the page. Then click the Add Details link that appears and follow steps 3–7 below. Doing so tells Facebook that your Group is hosting the Event and lets you invite all the Group's members in one fell swoop by turning on the checkbox next to "Invite Members of the host group [your Group's name]" that appears in the "Create an Event" box (see step 3).

Here's what you do:

1. **On the left side of your Home page, click the Events link**.

2. **On the Events page that appears, click the "Create an Event" button**.

3. **On the "Create an Event" page, fill out as many of the fields as possible**. You *have* to fill out some fields—like the Event's name (which you enter in the "What are you planning?" field)—but you should fill in as many of the others as you can. Doing so will make the Event easier for people to find, because they can search on every word you add. It also encourages people to RSVP, since the more people know about an Event (and the better you make it sound), the more likely they are to attend.

 Note Make sure you give your Event a name you like, because after you create your Event, you can't change what it's called. (You can, however, delete the Event and create a new one with a different name.)

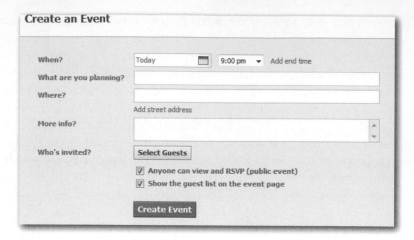

4. **Invite some guests**. When you click the Select Guests button, Facebook pops up a box that lists your friends and Friend Lists (page 63), so all you need to do is choose who you want to invite and then click "Save and Close".

 Facebook Events are supposed to be for your friends (or for the members of Groups you're in charge of—see page 112). So you can't invite Facebook members to Events unless they're your friends—but you *can* invite pals who aren't yet Facebook members. To do so, in the Select Guests box, head to the "Invite by E-mail Address" field and type in email addresses separated by commas, and then click "Save and Close."

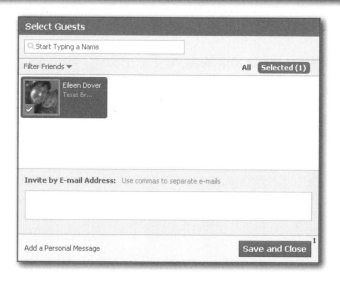

5. **Decide how open you want your Event to be**. Facebook assumes you want to plan a public Event that everyone on the site can view and attend. If that's fine with you—for example, if your Event is one that's open to the public and is listed in the local newspapers, or is an attend-in-spirit-only kind of shindig—you don't have to do a thing. Otherwise, you need to turn off the "Anyone can view and RSVP (public event)" checkbox. If you don't want potential attendees to know who else is already attending (perhaps you're organizing a surprise party, for example) turn off the "Show the guest list on the event page" checkbox.

 Tip For most face-to-face Events, you'll want to turn off the public event checkbox so you don't get a bunch of riffraff showing up.

6. **If you want, add a picture to your Event**. Technically, this step is optional, but an appropriate and clever photo, drawing, or logo will make your Event's listing a lot more appealing. To add a picture, click the Add Event Photo button on the left side of the "Create an Event" page.

7. **Click the Create Event button**. Facebook posts the Event so people can find it in searches (unless you made the Event private, that is).

You can change your Event after you create it. First, display the Event's profile (on the left side of your Home page, click the Events link and then, when the list of your Events appears, click the name of the Event you want to change). Then, on the right side of the Event's profile page, click the Edit Event link to change details, add a photo (click the Add Event Photo button), or cancel the Event. To invite additional folks: On the Event's profile page, click the "Select Guests to Invite" button.

Chapter 8
Going Shopping

As part of its quest to be the only website you ever need to visit, Facebook partnered with Oodle (a company that specializes in online classifieds) a while back to come up with an easy way for Facebook members to buy and sell stuff from each other. The result: An amped-up third-party application called Marketplace that replaces the original, built-in Facebook Marketplace feature. (The term "third-party" just means it was created by someone other than the programmers at Facebook.)

The Marketplace application is easy to find and add to your Facebook Account. And unlike the classifieds in your local paper or ads on *Craigslist.org* or eBay, on Facebook, you can comb through listings placed by friends, friends of friends, or fellow coworkers or students. And if you don't personally know the person who placed the ad, you can learn about him *before* you contact him. As you'll see in this chapter, you can use Facebook Marketplace to buy or sell just about anything.

 Note Marketplace still isn't quite the seller-packed, go-to shopping haunt that eBay is—*yet*. What it *is* spectacularly useful for is facilitating local sales: those Chihuahua puppies you want to get rid of, those textbooks gathering dust in the corner, that on-campus job you want to fill. Anything of special interest to your friends or fellow network members is a prime candidate for Marketplace.

The Marketplace Application

Marketplace is a Facebook *application* (see Chapter 12) that lets you post and answer want ads. You can use it to advertise that you want to rent a house, fill a position, sell a sofa—anything you're either looking for or looking to get rid of.

Because you get to choose a location to advertise in when you create a Marketplace ad (called a *listing*), the ads you see are ones you're most likely to want to respond to. So if you browse through all the Marketplace ads associated with San Francisco, you won't see ads for garage sales in New York.

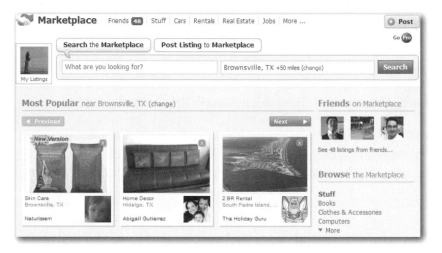

Note Marketplace doesn't accept ads for illegal or distasteful stuff like illicit drugs, explosives, or hate-group paraphernalia. You can see the list of banned items by heading to the left side of your Home page, clicking the Marketplace link (you may have to click the More link first), scrolling down to the bottom of the page that appears, and then clicking the "Terms of Use" link. On the left side of the page that appears, click "Prohibited Content". (You also get a chance to peruse these guidelines by clicking the "Terms of Service" link that appears in the "Request for Permission" box—see step 5 on page 134—when you give Marketplace access to your Facebook info.)

The Friend Factor: Ads from Facebook Connections

Thanks to the social-networking info it tracks (who's friends with whom), Facebook takes the concept of personal ads a step further than your average classifieds section or even the uber-popular free listing site *Craigslist.org*. Using the Facebook Marketplace application, you can:

- **Search through just your friends' (or fellow network members') listings**. Given a choice, most people would rather do business with friends than strangers. Marketplace gives you two ways of doing just that: using the Friends link at the top of the Marketplace home page, and—depending on how your friends placed their ads—combing through ads on your friends' Walls.

- **Feel out a seller by seeing the friends you have in common**. Sure, that "roommate wanted" ad sounds good, but before you contact the guy, wouldn't it be nice to contact a couple of mutual friends and find out what he's really like? Step 2 on page 138 explains how.

 Note Because its strength is putting a friendly face on ads, Marketplace is a great place to post ads you wouldn't want to put in the newspaper, like "Wanted: Help Moving" or "Need someone to feed my parrot while I'm on vacation." On the downside, because all your Facebook pals can see your ads, you might not want to use Marketplace to offload that chartreuse, monogrammed waffle maker your best friend gave you for your birthday.

Cost: Free, Risk: Yours

For now, Marketplace is fee free: There's no charge for placing a regular ad or answering one. When you answer an ad, it's your responsibility to contact the seller and work out payment arrangements—Facebook isn't involved in that and neither are the folks who created the Marketplace application. So be careful: If you pay someone for his beer stein collection but he takes the money and runs, you're on your own.

 Note If you sell stuff for a living—like real estate or cars, for example—you can fork over $25 a month (or thereabouts) for special Marketplace business listings. For details: On the Marketplace home page (*http://apps.facebook.com/marketplace*), click the "Go Pro" button that's just below the Post button.

Finding and Viewing Marketplace

Before you can buy, sell, or even look at stuff on Marketplace, you first have to find it.

If you ever used Facebook's original, built-in Marketplace feature, you'll find the new Marketplace application already listed on the left side of your Home page (you may have to click the More link to see it). Facebook made the switch to the new version quietly, behind the scenes, so members wouldn't have to do extra work.

If you don't see a Marketplace link, you need to find the Marketplace application. Here's how:

1. **In the Search box at the top of your screen, type *Marketplace* and then click the magnifying-glass icon**.

2. **On the search results page that appears, click the Marketplace logo, which looks like two hands shaking**. If you don't see it, try clicking the Apps link on the left side of the screen to narrow your results to just applications.

3. **On the Marketplace profile page that appears, click the "Go to App" button in the upper-left part of the screen**. Facebook whisks you to the Marketplace home page, shown on page 130.

 After you use Marketplace a certain number of times, Facebook **bookmarks** it for you, which means showing it on the left side of your Home page. Facebook's top-secret algorithms decide what "a certain number" is, and you can no longer bookmark applications yourself. So if you're hunting for the Marketplace application a couple days from now and it doesn't appear automatically on the left side of your Home page, simply type the word **Marketplace** into the Search box at the top of your screen and then hit Enter.

Placing an Ad

Placing a Marketplace ad (technically called a *listing*) is pretty straightforward, whether you want to find something, get rid of something, or get a job. You don't have to pay anything to place an ad, and it runs for 30 days.

To place a Marketplace ad:

1. **On the left side of your Home page, click the Marketplace link**. You may have to click the More link to see it. If you still don't see it, type "Marketplace" into the Search box at the top of the page and then hit Enter.

2. **On the Marketplace home page that appears, click the orange Post button**. Facebook displays the "Post a Listing" box.

3. **Choose a category for your listing.** Your choices are pretty straightforward: Stuff, Vehicle, Rentals, Houses, Jobs, Services, and Tickets. Once you pick a category from the drop-down list, you see a few radio buttons related to that category. Turn on the one that best matches your situation, and then click Continue. Marketplace displays a new box to include new fields related to the category you selected.

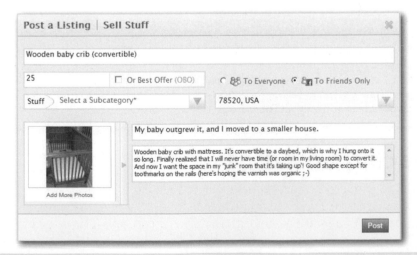

4. **Fill in as many details as you can and then click Post**. As you would when running an ad in the paper, make sure your description is as enticing and complete as possible. Include multiple photos if you can, because the placeholder image Marketplace gives you screams "The stuff I'm selling is in such bad shape I'm embarrassed to show it." (After you upload one photo, the Add A Photo link changes to read Add More Photos.)

 Because everybody on the Internet—not just Facebook members, but *everybody*—can see your Marketplace listing if it happens to come up in a web search, be careful about including sensitive info such as your phone number or home address. Besides, you really don't need to include that stuff anyway, because any Facebook member can get in touch with you by clicking the Respond button in your ad.

5. **In the "Request for Permission" box that pops up, click the Allow button to publish your ad.** Click Don't Allow instead if you want to wait on publishing (perhaps you want to go over your ad for errors one more time, or see if the phone call that's coming in right now is your neighbor calling to take the item off your hands).

 You see a similar "Request for Permission" box when you do other things on Marketplace, too. Using any Facebook application—including Marketplace—means opening your account up to non-Facebook employees. Unless you're extremely conservative when it comes to sharing your information, this isn't a big deal; still, it *does* pose a risk. (Chapter 12 has more details.) So if you're comfortable with Marketplace having access to your Facebook account, click the Allow button.

6. **Verify your email address**. To help cut down on spam and fake listings, before Facebook posts your ad on Marketplace, it asks you to confirm your email address by signing into your email account and clicking the link in the email Facebook sent you. When you do, you get whisked back to Facebook, where you see a message announcing that you've confirmed your address and your ad will show up in Marketplace soon.

 Facebook won't post your ad without verifying your email address. But sometimes—if you're giving stuff away (as opposed to selling it), for example—you may not see a confirmation box. If a confirmation box doesn't appear, check your Facebook inbox. Alternatively, in the upper left of the Marketplace home page, click the tiny blue My Listings link that appears beneath the thumbnail of your profile picture; doing so gives you an opportunity to tell Facebook to re-send the verification email.

7. **Double-check your listing and, if necessary, edit it**. If you spot a goof or decide to add a photo, you can edit your listing by clicking the Edit Details link below your listing description.

8. **Decide how (or if) you want to call extra attention to your listing**. Marketplace gives you three ways to make your ad stand out from the crowd:

— **Promoting your ad**. Because the ads folks see in their Marketplace search results appear in order from newest to oldest, when you post your ad, it zooms to the top of the search results—at first. (If 60 other people decide to sell *their* old treadmills the day after you placed your ad, your treadmill ad gets buried.) To scoot your ad back to the top of the heap temporarily, click the "Promote to Top of Results" link. You get to repeat this process once every 24 hours for as long as your ad runs.

- **Sharing your ad with friends.** If you think one or two of your Facebook friends will be especially interested in your ad, you can send it to them via email. Or, if you prefer, you can post your ad on your Wall for all your friends to check out. To do either, click Marketplace on your Home page and then click My Listings. Then, in the box that appears, click the name of the add you want to share, and then click the Share button on the ad itself.

- **Purchasing a Facebook ad.** By clicking the "Create an Ad" link that appears in the Sponsored section on the right side of your Home page, you can create a Facebook ad (Chapter 13) to help drive traffic to your listing.

Changing Your Ad

You place a Marketplace ad and then it hits you: You forgot to add an important detail. No problem! The Marketplace application makes it easy to:

- **View your listing.** To see a listing you've created, on the left side of your Home page, click Marketplace (you may have to click More first); then, on the Marketplace home page, click the My Listings link that appears under the thumbnail version of your profile picture. To see all the details of a listing, click its name.

- **Edit your listing.** You can change your ad any time. First, view the details of the ad as described above. Then, simply click the Edit Details link. In the Edit Your Listing box that appears, make your changes, and then click the Post button.

- **Close your listing.** To *close* (cancel) your listing, click Marketplace on your Home page, and then click the My Listings link. Then find the ad you want to delete and click Close. In the confirmation box that appears, turn on either the Yes radio button (if you're removing the ad because you sold the item) or the No radio button (if you're deleting the ad for some other reason), and then click Close Listing. If you change your mind after you close the listing, click the Activate link that Facebook displays in the ad's listing on your All Listings page.

Finding Stuff

Marketplace gives you several ways to find stuff you're looking for. From the Marketplace home page (get there by heading to the left side of your Home page and clicking Marketplace), you can:

- **See ads your friends, *their* friends, or your fellow network members have placed**. On the Marketplace home page, click the Friends link near the top of the page. Then head to the Posted By section on the left side of the page that appears and click All Friends & Networks, Friends, Friends & Friends-of-Friends, or the name of one of your networks.

- **Browse listings by location**. To see listings in or around a particular city, on the Marketplace home page, click the "change" link in the location box (the field just to the left of the Search button). Then fill out the dialog box that pops up and click Set Location.

- **Browse listings by category**. There's no point in seeing ads for homes for sale if you need a job. To see all the job listings associated with a specific location (see previous bullet), click one of the category listings on the right side of the Marketplace home page.

Note To see the stuff your friends have listed by category: On the Marketplace home page, click Friends. Then simply select one of the category tabs that appears on the left. If you're looking for a job, for example, click the Jobs tab. (If none of your friends have any current listings, you won't see any tabs.)

- **Search for an item within a category**. Depending on the category you choose (see previous bullet), you may see subcategories listed on the left side of the search results page, along with boxes you can use to narrow your search by entering minimum and maximum prices.

 Note Facebook encourages its members to be their brothers' keepers. If you run across an ad that rubs you the wrong way—whether it's for Nazi memorabilia or is just in the wrong category—click the "learn more" link in the Stop Scam section on the left side of any listing to send the Marketplace team a heads-up.

Answering an Ad

For privacy reasons, Marketplace listings rarely include direct contact info like phone numbers. Instead, you answer an ad by sending a Facebook message. Here's how:

1. **Search Marketplace to find what you're looking for, and then click the name of the listing you want to respond to**. Facebook displays the full ad, complete with pictures (if the person who placed it supplied any, that is).

2. **Do a quick reality check**. Scroll down to the Comments section of the ad's page and see if any other prospective buyers have asked questions (and how the person who listed the ad answered). Then click the View My Facebook Profile link below the picture of the person who listed the ad; this sends you to her profile, which you can browse to get a feel for whether you want to conduct business with her. Any friends you have in common with the ad lister appear in the Mutual Friends section of the lister's profile. If you have a mutual friend, it couldn't hurt to ask that person about the lister before you respond to the ad.

Note If you're the kind of person who likes to get a little feedback from friends before making a big investment, you might want to click the Share button that appears near the bottom of every Marketplace listing. Doing so lets you email your query ("Is this a good deal?")—along with a link to the ad you're considering—to whichever friends you think will give you the best advice. To send the email, in the box that pops up, click the "Send as a Message instead" link.

3. **If the person's profile page checks out, answer the ad.** Click your web browser's back button, and then click the big green Respond button. Then, in the New Message box that appears, fill out the Message field and click Send.

Chapter 9
Hiring and Getting Hired

In real life, people hire and fire based on info they get through the grape-vine—in other words, through their social networks: "You're looking for a programmer? My brother-in-law's the best programmer on the planet! Here's his number." Or, "They're hiring down at my gym. You should throw them a resumé."

Because Facebook's whole *raison d'être* is social networking, it should come as no surprise that the site can be a big help in job searches. This chapter shows you how to work the job pool from both angles: If you're looking for an employee or intern, you can use Facebook to recruit and vet prospects. If you're job hunting, you can use the site to research jobs and make connections with people who might help you get hired.

Recruiting New Hires

Facebook's recruiting options range from free to spendy. Deciding up front who you want to target (recent college grads with specific degrees? Seasoned employees at rival firms? Anyone in the greater tri-state area with a pulse?) can help you choose the options best suited for your particular situation. The following sections explain various ways of headhunting on Facebook.

Creating a Recruitment Page

Even if your company already has a corporate Facebook Page, if you do a lot of year-round hiring you should consider creating an additional free Page devoted to recruitment (page 176 shows you how).

When you create your recruitment Page:

- **Put the word "careers" in the Page's title**. Or "jobs," or some other word that helps potential recruits (and employment-related Facebook applications [see page 144]) quickly find your Page and understand its purpose.

- **Create different sections for different types of recruits (page 178)**. Separating info for recent college grads from the stuff for experienced hires, for example, helps your audience locate relevant info quickly and makes it easier for you to update your Page.

- **Pack your Page with relevant company- and employee-related info**. Don't stop with text and links to your corporate HR site; add photos and video clips that help job seekers envision themselves working for you.

- **Do things on your Page frequently**. Each time you post a job opening, schedule an Event such as a hiring fair (see Chapter 7), or take some other action on your Page, would-be recruits who've "liked" your Page (see page x) get notified instantly.

Paid Advertising

Social ads (page 181) let you advertise job openings to potential employees who meet specific criteria—for example, folks with certain degrees or job skills who live in specific geographic areas.

Posting a Marketplace Ad

One of the first things a job hunter will likely check is the Facebook Marketplace. Happily, posting a "help wanted" ad in the Marketplace is quick and easy; see page 132 for details.

When you're creating your listing, be sure to click the "Select a subcategory" drop-down list. Then spend some time figuring out which subcategory best matches the position you're trying to fill. You should also choose an item from the Job Type drop-down menu (click the "Add company and job type (optional)" field to display it). That lets you make it clear whether the position is a regular, full-time, paid position or some variation such as part-time, internship, or contract work.

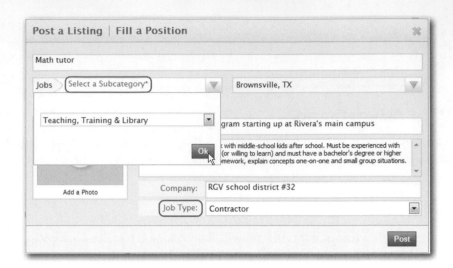

Working with a Recruiting Firm

Scads of recruiting firms have set up shop on Facebook. Some maintain Pages that include up-to-date job listings; others have created Facebook applications that job seekers can use to search multiple employers' openings and receive automated notifications of job listings that match the skills and interests they've listed on their Facebook profiles.

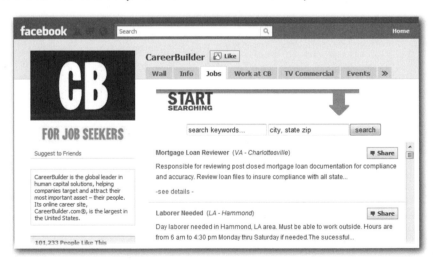

Each recruiting firm and application is different, and each has different requirements and terms for advertising your company's job postings, so you'll need to contact the ones you're interested in. To find a list of the recruiting firms currently on Facebook, type a phrase such as *recruiting firm* or *careers* into the Search box at the top of any Facebook screen and then, at the bottom of the drop-down list that appears, click the "See more results" link. To find a list of employment-related Facebook applications, type *jobs* or *job search* into the Search box instead; then, on the left side of the search results page that appears, click the Apps link.

Searching for Prospects

Not everyone tells the truth on Facebook, but people looking for jobs generally do. These folks often pack their profiles with professional details, such as their current job title, the company they work for, and even their skills and interests. (See page 150 for more on using your profile as a resumé.) In earlier versions of Facebook, you could search for prospective hires using an advanced search feature that let you hunt for specific skills and interests, but that feature is long gone. Now your search options include:

- Working with one of the recruiting firms on Facebook that searches members' profiles for you—for a fee (page 144).

Tip If you're searching for someone with an unusual skill set or to fill a very specific position—like curriculum designer, say—you can try searching for Facebook members who've mentioned that skill set or gig in a recent post on their own profile. (Job seekers often do just that.) In the Search box at the top of any Facebook page, type in the position or skill set you're looking for and then click the "See results" link. Then head to the left side of the search results page that appears and click "Posts by Everyone".

- Installing and using a Facebook application (Chapter 12) such as Advanced Search 2.0 that offers fancy search features.

- Using a stripped-down version of the original Facebook search tool.

Tip To search for potential recruits who currently work for another company, point your browser to *www.facebook.com/srch.php*. On that page, scroll down to the "Search by Company" section, type in the company's name, and then click "Search for Coworkers".

Recruiting firms and Facebook search applications find member profiles in various ways. Searching using Facebook's built-in search tool is relatively straightforward, but won't return as targeted a list of prospects as the first two approaches listed above. To use Facebook's built-in search tool:

1. **Point your browser to *www.facebook.com/search.php*.**

2. **Type in a school or workplace, or type an email address or name in the Search box near the top of the screen that appears (the one to the right of the All Results heading).** When you finish, click the magnifying glass on the right side of the Search box.

3. **Comb through the results, check out the most promising people's profiles, and contact the folks you're interested in**.

 Because Facebook has been systematically de-emphasizing its own search feature in favor of search applications, don't be surprised if the site yanks its search tool at some point.

Announcing an Opening to Your Friends

Facebook's real strength is the way it connects you to other people through friends and acquaintances you have in common—and you don't even need to spend an evening at a cocktail party to get in touch with them. Here's how to get the most out of an offhand mention that you're looking to hire:

- **Make sure your privacy settings are letting the buzz through**. See page 219 for guidance on adjusting your News Feed and privacy settings. At the very least, set the "Posts by me" option to "Friends of Friends". Take a look at your "Apps and Websites" privacy settings, too, and turn on the checkboxes next to any items you plan to use to communicate your opening (such as "Info accessible through your friends" and "Public search").

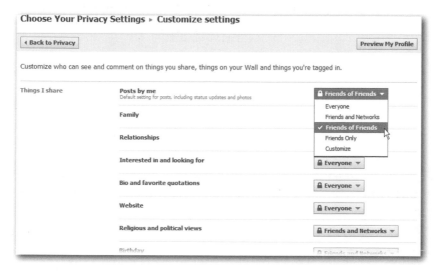

- **Mention the job opening on your Wall or on one of your friends' Walls**. Be specific (and succinct—under 20 words is best) about the type of candidate you're looking for. Not only does your post stay on the Wall for prospective recruits to find, but your friends (or your Page's fans, if you've created a Facebook Page) all see your brief description in their News Feeds.

- **If you or someone else at your company created a Marketplace listing, share it**. Clicking the Share button in the middle of any Marketplace listing lets you post the official job description on your profile or email it directly to people you think might be interested. This kind of fishing expedition is so unobtrusive it's guaranteed not to cause hard feelings. And if one of your friends is interested in the job—or knows someone who is—they know how to get in touch with you.

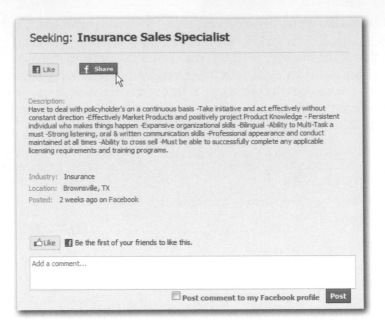

Seeking: **Insurance Sales Specialist**

Like | f Share

Description:
Have to deal with policyholder's on a continuous basis -Take initiative and act effectively without constant direction -Effectively Market Products and positively project Product Knowledge - Persistent individual who makes things happen -Expansive organizational skills -Bilingual -Ability to Multi-Task a must -Strong listening, oral & written communication skills -Professional appearance and conduct maintained at all times -Ability to cross sell -Must be able to successfully complete any applicable licensing requirements and training programs.

Industry: Insurance
Location: Brownsville, TX
Posted: 2 weeks ago on Facebook

Like | f Be the first of your friends to like this.

Add a comment...

☐ Post comment to my Facebook profile | Post

 Note You can also share job listings that are posted on your company's website. To do so: At the top of your Wall, click the Link button (it's to the right of the word "Share"). In the space that appears, type in the URL where folks can find the complete job description, application, or what-have-you, and then click the Attach button. Then type a brief "Let me know if you know someone who would be a good fit for this gig" message in the "Say something about this link" field that appears. To get the word out to the most people, click the padlock-shaped privacy icon and select Everyone. When you finish, click Share.

- **Consider using an employment-related Facebook application**. Applications such as Workin' It! help you get the word out that you're looking for a new hire. Page 144 shows you how to search for employment-related applications.

 Tip You can also try posting a quickie job announcement on an appropriate business Group's discussion board—a discussion board hosted on one of the old Facebook Groups devoted to business, that is. See Chapter 6 for more info.

Vetting Prospects

Running online background checks on potential candidates—especially for high-tech and computer-related jobs—is practically de rigueur these days: It's cheap, quick, and eye-opening in ways that formal interviews and resumés aren't.

It takes all of 5 minutes to conduct a Facebook background check on a candidate: Just head to the Search box at the top of any Facebook page, type the person's name, and either click the matching name that appears, or click the "See more results" link and continue combing through the search results until you hit paydirt.

 Tip For the complete scoop on searching, flip to page 47.

The profile that appears may or may not contain the truth, the whole truth, and nothing but the truth about the person—but it probably tells you *something* useful. In addition to obvious red flags (like pictures of the candidate passed out naked), check for mutual friends who may be able to give you candid feedback about the prospect. (If you have friends in common, a "You and So-and-so" section appears on the right side of the person's profile page.)

 Note Clicking the Share Profile link at the bottom left of someone's profile lets you send that person's profile info to other members of your hiring team.

Note that Facebook's privacy settings let folks hide some of their profile details. If this is the case for a prospect you're interested in, click the "Add as Friend" button that appears at the top of her profile page. After the prospect befriends you, you should be able to see a lot more of her profile.

 Tip If you're having trouble finding a candidate on Facebook but have reason to believe he's a member, check with your company's HR department to see if there's anyone on staff who happens to share the candidate's alma mater or former employer. If so, that person should be able to access the prospect's profile, since he's eligible to join the prospect's Facebook networks.

Looking for a Job

Facebook is a terrific tool for anyone searching for a gig. Not only can you use your profile as a combination multimedia resumé/portfolio, but you can also use Facebook to network *and* tap into your friends' expertise and contacts. Read on to learn how.

 Tip A quick search of Facebook's Application Directory (page 198) for "jobs" and "employment" yields dozens of Facebook applications designed to help you land gainful employment. Some you might find useful include My LinkedIn Profile (if you use the business-oriented social network LinkedIn, you can use this application to add your job-focused LinkedIn profile to your Facebook profile); Extended Info (which lets you add additional career-focused facts, like accomplishments and awards, to your Facebook profile); and NetworkedBlogs (good if you regularly write industry-related blogs, because it lets you import those blogs into your Facebook profile). Chapter 12 shows you how to find and install applications.

Turning Your Profile into a Resumé

If you're serious about making Facebook part of your job hunt, the first thing to do is assume that every potential hiring manager can see your *whole* profile, and build (or clean up) your profile accordingly. You don't want your dream job to slip through your fingers because of a stupid comment, a way-too-candid photo, or a Page listed on your profile that celebrates illegal activities, for example. Maybe you mean it all as a joke, but that doesn't matter: If you have an unprofessional profile, a hiring manager will take one look at it and see, at the very least, poor judgment and a total lack of understanding of how the Web works.

 Note Chapter 13 shows you several ways to hide profile info, but it also explains why you can't trust that the information will *stay* hidden.

Here are some ways to spiff up your profile to help you land a job:

- **Edit your profile info**. At the top right of any Facebook page, click Profile, and then click the Info link on the left side of the screen. Then the Edit link to the right of any section's header to tweak it. Fill out the "Education and Work" section completely, using all the industry buzzwords you can in the Description field. Also, describe your job-related skills in the "Activities and Interests" section. Because these fields are easy for potential employers to search, pack them with descriptions of your technical abilities and interpersonal skills.

- **Do work-related stuff on Facebook**. Post regular, impressive Notes that relate to your current job or job-related interests; start a work-related Page; hold work-related Events; upload samples of your work, such as reports, slideshows, video or audio clips, photos, or applications you've written; and befriend as many industry movers and shakers as you can.

- **Present yourself professionally**. Keep the silly astrology and zombie applications (see Chapter 12) to a minimum, choose your friends carefully, and don't write anything on anybody's Wall (or "Like" a Page) that you wouldn't feel comfortable writing on a whiteboard at work.

- **Edit your Notifications preferences so you know when your friends share your links with *their* friends (page 90)**. This will alert you to potential contacts. Surf to your friend's friend's profile, read up on her, and—if appropriate—approach her as a "friend of a friend." (As in, send her a polite Message [page 70]; *don't* poke her! Poking isn't very professional—see page 77.)

- **Don't assume that potential employers *won't* be able to access your networks or profile**. In all probability, they can and will (see Chapter 13).

Using the Marketplace

Facebook hopes its Marketplace (described in Chapter 8) will become the go-to place for jobs (and sofas, and roommates, and all the other transactions that make up day-to-day life). The Marketplace is much beefier than it was just a couple years ago, but it's still a little skimpy on bona fide job listings, so sites like *Monster.com* and *Craigslist.org* probably aren't feeling particularly threatened just yet. Still, it's worth spending some time checking out the Marketplace. At the very least:

- **Browse Marketplace Jobs**. It takes only a few seconds to see whether the Marketplace lists any openings in your area and field. To scope things out, click the Marketplace link on the left side of your Home page (you may have to click the More link first to see it). At the top of the Marketplace page that appears, click the Jobs link.

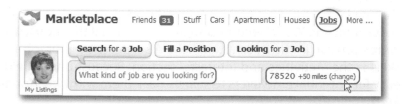

The Jobs page that appears displays a bunch of listings. To see only specific types of jobs, head to the left-hand side of the page and click the subcategory you're interested in.

 Note You can browse—and search—jobs in other cities, too. Here's how: On the Marketplace Jobs page, click the "change" link that's in the second search field near the top of the page. Then, in the Location dialog box that appears, type a city's name in the middle field. When Facebook's list of suggestions pops up (you see it if you type slowly), choose a city, and then click the Submit button. Now, when you browse or search for jobs, Facebook browses or hunts in that new location.

- **Search Marketplace Jobs**. If you know precisely what you're after— a specific job title, location, or company, for example—you can get quicker results by *searching* Marketplace than by browsing it. To search Marketplace jobs, head to the main Marketplace Jobs page (see previous bullet), type the job you're looking for in the first field at the top of the screen (the one with the "Search for a Job" balloon pointing at it), and then hit Enter to see listings that match your criteria.

 Note Because some of the jobs listed on Marketplace were pulled from professional job sites, job hunting on Marketplace may introduce you to helpful job sites you never knew existed. In Marketplace's job listings, check for jobs displaying a "Posted on [some job site]" label and then—whether or not the actual job sounds like something you want to pursue—click the job's title and check out the website that appears.

- **Post a "Looking for Work" ad**. While it's probably not the fastest route to a new gig, creating a "Here are my qualifications and what I'm looking for" listing in Marketplace couldn't hurt—and it's easy to do: Click the Marketplace link on the left side of your Home page and then click the Post link at the top of the main Marketplace page. In the "Post a Listing" box that appears, select Jobs from the drop-down menu. Then, turn on the radio box next to "Looking for a Job" and click Continue. Type the title and a concise, meaty description of the role you want, and don't forget to provide an explanation in the "Why are you the right hire?" field. If the location that appears in the last field *isn't* the spot where you're hoping to find a job, click that field and type a new location in the pop-up box that appears. Double-check that the radio button next to Everyone is turned on (since the more folks who see your ad, the better). When you're all done, click the Post button to create your listing.

Networking

Networking—finding out who knows who and letting all of 'em know what you have to offer—is what Facebook is all about. Here are a couple of ways you can put your networking skills to good use in your job search:

- **Attend industry-related Events**. Doing so shows the world you're truly interested in your line of work. It also gives you the opportunity to network in person and stay current on what's happening in your field. Some large employers and some job shops (such as CareerBuilder) offer online and face-to-face hiring fairs, too. Often, you find hiring fairs listed in the Events tab of an employer's or job shop's Facebook profile.

- **Let your friends know you're looking**. Instead of just sending private messages, consider tweaking your Feed preferences and then writing a brief note on your Wall about the kind of job you want (see page 78).

Chapter 10
Collaborating on Projects via Facebook

xpensive groupware, workflow management tools, and other collaboration programs have been around for quite a while. With its open-door policy and privacy concerns (see Chapter 13), Facebook is certainly no replacement for a dedicated, bulletproof collaboration program like Lotus Domino or Novell Groupwise. But you might find that some of Facebook's tools are handy—and free—ways to help your team get work done quickly. This chapter gives Facebook's messaging and subscription tools (which Chapters 4–7 introduced you to) a decidedly business-like spin. You'll see how to use them to keep team members, coworkers, and clients in the loop—and projects on track.

> **Note** Some employers block access to social networking sites such as Facebook. The top two reasons? Loss of productivity and security concerns such as those explained in Chapter 13. If your company won't let you use Facebook at work, you can probably skip this chapter—unless you want to collaborate on non-work projects using the site.

Keeping in Touch

The same Facebook features that let you and your friends "talk" online—Messages (page 69), Events (Chapter 7), Groups (Chapter 6), Friend Lists (page 63), Chat (page 76), and Notes (page 67)—can help you keep up to date with coworkers, clients, and customers. The features work the same way whether you're interacting with your old college roommate or your boss. But there are a few things you need to keep in mind when you're using these features for work:

- **Professionalism**. Email has done more to lower professional communication standards than casual Friday ever did. And now that everyone is finally used to emoticons, here comes Facebook, a site so hip, hot, and happening—and easy to use—that it doesn't just encourage you to be informal; it practically *orders* you to. The thing is, you never know who might view your Facebook exploits, even if you're scrupulous about privacy (see Chapter 13). So, instead of thinking of Facebook as an employee lunchroom, think of it as a meeting that the big brass might drop in on at any time. Keep personal info, off-color jokes, and just-for-fun applications (Chapter 12) to a bare minimum.

- **Privacy**. If you're using Facebook for business, you'll want to scale back the Notifications the site sends out about your activities. That way your boss won't get barraged with details of, say, your love life. In particular, you want to adjust your privacy settings (Chapter 13).

- **Security**. Be careful not to discuss anything mission-critical on Facebook, and don't post confidential company documents of any kind. And because you can't be sure that info you give the site won't get out, you may even want to keep mum about things like your work phone number and travel itinerary.

Sending Messages

Whether you're an employee working in a cubicle farm or a freelancer working from home, you've probably already got an email program. So, why use Facebook to send and receive Messages? Two reasons:

- **It's super easy**. If your coworkers and clients are on Facebook, sending them a Message takes only one click—whether you want to invite them to an impromptu meeting, comment on a document or website one of them posted, or share a video clip. (Thank the "Send [somebody] a Message", "Share," and other click-to-contact links scattered around the site.)

If some of your coworkers and clients aren't on Facebook, page 53 explains an easy way to invite them to join.

- **It helps you organize your correspondence.** If your team uses Facebook to collaborate on a project, Facebook's messaging feature helps you keep project-specific correspondence separate from your other work-related email.

Setting Up Meetings

Intranets (private websites that only company employees can access) are great for lining up in-house meetings, but Facebook *Events* are a handy way to organize get-togethers that involve a mix of coworkers and "civilians" such as clients, potential clients, suppliers, and former employees.

 For the full scoop on Events, flip to Chapter 7.

The thing you want to pay attention to when organizing an Event is the level of access that you grant other people (see page 122). So after you click the Events link on the left side of your Home page and then click the "Create an Event" button to display the "Create an Event" page, do the following:

- **Turn off the checkbox next to "Anyone can view and RSVP (public event)".** Doing so keeps details of your Event out of non-attendees' searches and News Feeds.

- **Decide how much access to grant attendees**. If it's a relatively open meeting and you want attendees to be able to invite their own staff, customers, and so on, turn on the checkbox next to "Guests can invite Friends." (Just keep in mind that doing so might let the cat out of the bag, News Feed-wise; if you really want a private event, keep this checkbox turned off.) If you don't want anyone to know who's attending the meeting—say it's a sales meeting and you don't want your attendees to get together without you before you've had a chance to give your official pitch—turn off the "Show the guest list on the event page" checkbox.

Exchanging Ideas

Facebook *Pages* (page 174) are great for user groups and other customer-oriented information exchanges. You get to combine your company's logo with Facebook's groovy collaboration features (such as a comment board, the ability to exchange files, and one-click messaging to all Page fans) to build or maintain interest in your company and products—for free!

Another option is using Facebook's new *Groups* (Chapter 6), which are terrific for:

- **Keeping team members up-to-date**. If your company doesn't have an intranet and is relying instead on email for team discussions, you're going to love Facebook Groups. Using Groups is a lot easier than dealing with mile-long "me too" replies and CC lists—*and* Groups give people a single place to go for updates and file exchanges. Just be sure you make the Group secret (page 114) to keep important details out of the hands of riffraff (meaning anybody who's not a confirmed team member). You'll want to set up a Group email address, too, so team members working out of airports and hotels can participate in the Group even when they can't log into Facebook (page 112).

- **Holding real-time team discussions.** When you create a new Facebook Group and add all the members of your team to it, they get to use Facebook's Chat feature (page 110) to instant-message the whole Group all at once—perfect for double-checking that everyone got yesterday's memo or taking a quick vote.

- **Passing around documents for comments and changes.** Group members can create documents using Facebook's basic text editor (page 110). Once a document is created, any other Group member can open it and change it, similar to the way a wiki works.

 Note Unfortunately, you can't upload a document you've created in a word processing program, such as Microsoft Word, into Facebook and pass it around your Group. Only documents—or *Docs*, as Facebook calls them—created by a Group member in Facebook can be worked on by other Group members.

Chapter 6 has the lowdown on setting up and using Groups.

Creating and Subscribing to Notes

Facebook *Notes* (page 97) are basically blog entries people can subscribe to. You *could* use plain old email to send your team multimedia documents like project milestones, ongoing customer service requests, or meeting minutes. But using Notes instead gives team members the best of both worlds: Notifications (page 88) that alert them every time you post a new document, and a single, easily accessible archive of everything you've posted.

To use Notes:

- **"Friend" each team member you want to see your Notes (page 56).**

- **Adjust your Facebook settings so only your team members can see your Notes**. On the "Choose Your Privacy Settings - Customize settings" page (page 222), zip to the "Posts by me" setting and choose Customize, then type in the name of each person on your team.

- **Have your team members subscribe to your Notes**. Ask each of them to head to their Home pages and click the Notes link on the left side of the page (they may need to click the More link to see it), and then find a Note you've written. They should then click the title of the Note and, on the left side of the page that appears, click the "[Your Name]'s Notes" link. On the next page, they should click the "Subscribe to this feed" link. (See page 92 for more on subscribing to Feeds.)

Exchanging Files

It doesn't matter whether you're talking team meetings, sales conferences, or product launches: All business interactions generate documents. Brochures, diagrams, attendee lists, action items, reports, flow charts—the list goes on and on. Fortunately, one of the things Facebook excels at is letting you exchange files painlessly and privately.

 Note Privacy, of course, is relative. No free site will ever guard your data as carefully as you would. See Chapter 13 for the scoop on Facebook privacy. The bottom line: Don't use Facebook to send confidential info.

Facebook's built-in Photos application lets you upload and share image files with your coworkers. And the built-in Links application lets you share just about anything else, from audio and video clips to files and documents stored on the Web. Read on to learn how, or flip to page 195 to learn about applications.

Sharing Pictures

You can use Facebook's Photos application to upload and share image files. The files you upload have to be in one of these three Internet-friendly formats: .jpg, .bmp, .png (with some restrictions that are explained in the next section), or .gif (but *not* animated GIFs).

Tip If you're not sure what format an image file is in, here's how to find out: Locate the file on your computer and right-click it (or Control-click it on a Mac); then select Properties (Get Info on a Mac) from the pop-up menu that appears. The info box you see lists the file's format.

On Facebook, you organize your picture files by grouping them into *albums*. You can limit access to each album so that only certain team members can see it, and you can even *tag* individual pictures within the album. (*Tagging* [page 166] is a way of associating one or more person with the picture, which is useful for establishing and tracking accountability. For example, you can tag a picture of a features list so that each list item is associated with the team member responsible for developing it.)

 Note Albums aren't the only way to share pictures. In addition to your profile picture, Facebook lets you add pictures to Groups, Events, and Notes. But using the Photos application's albums is your best bet when you want to keep project- or team-related photos, drawings, sketches, or screenshots in one place.

Creating and Filling an Album

Uploading and sharing a group of picture files is pretty straightforward Here's how to do it:

 Note You can share video clips as easily as you can share photos. To share a video clip, in step 2 of the following list, instead of clicking the Upload Photos button, click the Upload Video button. Then, on the page that appears, make sure the File Upload tab is selected and follow the instructions that appear. Facebook requests that any video clip you share is one that you or your friends shot, and that features either you or one (or more) of your friends. Because video files tend to be huge, you're limited to sharing only those files that weigh in at less than 1024 megabytes.

1. **On the left side of your Home page, click the Photos link (you may have to click the More link first to see it).**

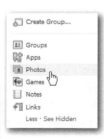

 Note Because Photos is an application, you can delete it (see page 205). If you deleted it by accident, turn to page 198 to learn how to find and reinstall it.

2. **On the Photos page that appears, click the Upload Photos button**. When you do, Facebook may display a Facebook Plug-In dialog box telling you that you have to install a *plug-in*—a tiny program that runs inside your web browser—to upload photos. (If you don't see this dialog box, skip to step 3.) If you decide not to install the plug-in, you can use an older version of Facebook's uploader tool called the Simple Uploader that only lets you upload a few images at a time. Installing the new plug-in is easy, so unless you almost never upload images, you're best off installing it.

   To install the plug-in: In the Facebook Plug-In dialog box, click Install, and then click the Download Facebook Plug-In link that appears. When you do, your computer asks where you want to save the downloaded file. Choose a spot you can remember (like on your desktop), and then save the file. Next, find the file on your computer, open it, choose your language, and then click OK. It takes only a few seconds for Facebook to install the file, and then it displays a dialog box confirming the installation. Back in your web browser, click the Done Installing button.

 Note If you're on a Mac, you may have trouble downloading and installing the plug-in. Happily, Facebook offers a separate plug-in that lets you send images from iPhoto right to Facebook. For details on how to install and use it, head to *http://developers. facebook.com/iphoto*.

3. **In the Upload Photos box, click the Select Photos button.**

4. **In the "Select files to upload" box that appears, tell Facebook which image files you want to upload**. The dialog box lets you comb through your computer's drives and choose the images you want. To select an image, simply click it; click it again to deselect it.

 Tip To select a bunch of contiguous images quickly, select the image at the top of the group and then press and hold the Shift key while you click on the image at the bottom of the bunch. Pressing Ctrl instead lets you select multiple noncontiguous images.

   The files you choose need to weigh in at less than 15 megabytes each. (See the Tip on page 161 for details about checking a photo's file format; the info box that appears also lists the file's size.) After you choose the files you want to upload, click the Open button, and Facebook takes you back to the Upload Photos dialog box.

5. **In the Upload Photos dialog box, describe your album, and then click Create Album**. Whatever you type in the Album Name and Location fields will be visible to everyone who can see your album, so keep it professional. (If you don't type in a name, Facebook uses today's date for the album's name.) Don't bother turning on the radio box next to High Resolution *unless* you expect folks to print the photos you're uploading; for viewing online, the Standard setting is just fine. From the Privacy drop-down list, choose Only Friends to restrict album access to just your team members.

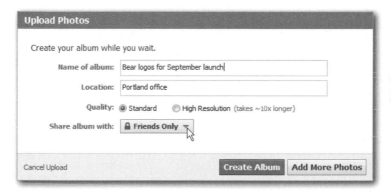

6. **Decide whether you want to publish your album right away**. If everything is all set, go ahead and click Publish Now. Or, if you don't want Facebook to alert your team members of your new images right away, click Skip. That way, you can sort through your photos, add a few captions, and make other changes before you let folks peek at your pictures. When you've got a fresh cup of joe and you're ready to make those adjustments, start editing your album as explained next.

Even if you click the Skip button (instead of the Publish Now button), people will still be able to see your images if they go hunting for them. As soon as you create an album, it shows up in the Photos section of your profile. By putting the publishing step off until later, you simply prevent Facebook from making a big announcement about your new album by posting it on your Wall and alerting your friends via their News Feeds.

After you scroll down and click Save Changes, Facebook gives you an opportunity to edit your album (click the Edit Album Info link at the bottom left of the screen) or add more photos (click the Add More Photos button that appears at the top right).

Editing Your Album

After you create an album, you can change practically anything about it. First, head to the My Uploads page: On the left side of your Home page, click the Photos link, and then click the My Uploads link that appears below it. On the My Uploads page, find the album you want to edit and then click the Edit Album link below its name. This takes you to a page dedicated to that album, where you can:

- **Delete pictures**. Click the Edit Photos tab if it's not already selected. Scroll to the picture you want to delete and turn on the "Delete this photo" checkbox below it. (To delete multiple pictures, turn on each picture's checkbox.) Then head to the bottom of the page and click the Save Changes button.

 To delete a whole album, click the Delete tab and then click the Delete button that appears.

- **Reorder your pictures**. Click the "Back to Album" link (it's at the top right of the page). On the page that appears, mouse over your pictures until you see a four-headed arrow, then drag the pictures into the order you want them.

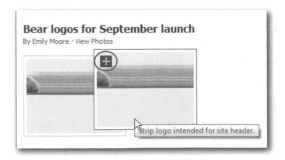

- **Add captions to pictures**. Click the Edit Photos tab, head to a picture, and then type your text into the Caption field. Don't forget to click Save Changes at the bottom of the screen when you're done.

 Caption text pops up when people mouse over a picture in an album.

- **Choose a picture to use as the album's "cover."** Facebook assumes you want the first picture you uploaded to be the album's cover, but you can tell it differently. To pick your own cover, scroll to the picture you want to appear as a thumbnail (a tiny image) wherever Facebook displays your album, such as in an email message you've attached the album to. Click the "This is the album cover" radio button below the photo of your choice, and then head to the bottom of the page and click Save Changes.
- **Change the name or description of your album**. Click the Edit Info tab, make your changes, and then click Save Changes.

 Saving your changes makes Facebook display a "Share this album with friends, even if they're not on Facebook" link—handy for sharing photos with someone without forcing them to register for Facebook. Simply click the link and type a recipient's name (if they're already on Facebook) or email address (if they're not) in the To field that appears, and then click Send Message.

- **Publish your album**. Click the Edit Photos tab and then click the Publish Now button to let folks see the results of your handiwork.

 To add more photos to an existing album, head to your My Uploads page (as explained at the beginning of this section), and then click the name of one of your albums. On the page that appears, click the Add More Photos button.

Viewing Your Album

After you create an album, Facebook displays a thumbnail of the album's cover in the Photos section of your profile (to see it, click the Photos link on the left side of your profile). Click an album to take a look at it. If you decide to make changes to it, click the Edit Album Info link on the album's page.

When someone else clicks the album's name, Facebook displays album info along with links to each picture in the album.

Everyone who can see your full profile can see your photos, but folks who can see your photos can't necessarily see your profile. That's because Facebook lets you set access to your profile and to your albums separately, as explained next.

Restricting Access to Your Albums

Facebook gives you pretty tight control over who can see your albums. You determined this when you created your album, but you can change this setting at any time: On the My Uploads page (page 164), find the album you want to tweak and click its Edit Album link, then click the Edit Info tab and choose one of the following from the Privacy drop-down list:

- **Everyone**
- **Friends and Networks**
- **Friends of Friends**
- **Friends Only**
- **Customize...** Clicking this option lets you specify particular friends or networks you want to see your album. This is useful if, for example, you've got a team of employees and contract workers and want certain photos to be visible only to one of the two groups. In this case, you can either grant viewing access to individual email addresses or a specific Friend List (page 63).

 Even if you restrict access to your albums to a specific group of Facebook friends, others may still be able see those pictures in the restricted album that you *tag* (see next section). To prevent news of your having tagged someone in a photo from showing up in a non-team-member's News Feed, customize the "Posts by me" privacy setting (page 147) to exclude any folks you want to hide the album from completely.

Tagging (Labeling) Your Pictures

Tagging is a nifty way to add virtual labels to your images. You can use tags to identify people in group pictures, and they're a handy way to indicate who's responsible for creating or working on something shown in a picture. For example, tagging each section of a flowchart or schematic with a coworker's name lets everyone know who's in charge of what, quickly and easily.

Every time someone looks at your photo album, he sees thumbnails of all the people tagged in that album. Clicking any photo in the album displays a list of the folks tagged in that photo.

Then, when he mouses over the tagged portion of a picture, up pops the taggee's name.

 Tip It's faster to wait until you finish your album to start tagging people.

To tag a picture:

1. **Head to the album's main page and then click the Tag Photos button.** To get to an album's main page from your Home page, click the Photos link (it's on the left side of the page), then the My Uploads link that appears, and finally the name of an album.

2. **In the text field that appears, type the first taggee's name.** As you type, Facebook displays a list of your friends; click to select the one you want.

3. **Mouse over the picture you want to tag.** Your cursor turns into crosshairs.

4. **When your cursor is right over the spot you want to tag, click.** Facebook draws a white square on the picture to show you which part of it will be associated with the person you selected. If you goof or change your mind about where to put the tag, double-click the picture to remove the white square and then click again.

5. **Repeat steps 2–4 as many times as you like.**

6. **When you finish, click the Save Tags button.**

Sharing Links and Other Items

If you can find a link to something on the Web, you can add it to your Facebook profile. Think company documents from your corporate site, video clips from your marketing department, or relevant research you've collected from all over the Web that you want your team to see. Depending on your privacy settings (Chapter 13), the items you post appear in your News Feed and on your Wall.

Team members can add their comments after they've checked out each item, and then share the items with others (even non-Facebook members) quickly and easily by clicking the Share button or link that appears alongside each posted item.

Best of all, multimedia links appear complete with controls so the people browsing your posted items can easily listen to music, watch a video clip, or check out other content you've posted.

To share something:

1. **At the top of your Home page or profile, click the appropriate icon for what you want to share: your status, a photo, a link, or a video.** If you're on your profile page, make sure the Wall link is selected on the left side of the page.

2. **Tell Facebook where to find the link (or other item) you want to share**. Follow the onscreen prompts to tell Facebook about the file or link. When you finish, click Attach (if you're sharing a link) and then click Share.

3. **Click the "Say something about this [item]" field and type a note explaining why you want your team to see this item**. From the web address you specified, Facebook automatically pulls in the title of the item, a description, and any pictures the web page contains. The title and description are usually pretty useful, but if you don't like one or both, simply click either one and start typing your own. Then use the arrow buttons to flip through the thumbnail pictures Facebook copied from the site you linked to and either choose an image you want to appear next to your posted link or turn on the No Thumbnail checkbox.

Tip To share something only with your team members (and *not* clutter your own Wall), click the padlock icon next to the Share button and choose Customize; then—from the "These people" drop-down list—choose Specific People. In the text field that appears, type the name of the Friend List containing your team members, or just type in your team members' names one by one.

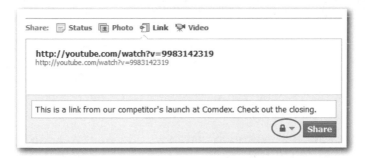

4. **Click Share**. The item appears on your Wall. In addition, depending on your privacy settings (see Chapter 13), news of your newly posted item may also appear in your friends' News Feeds.

Tip To delete an item you've posted, head to your Wall or News Feed, mouse over the item, and then click the X that appears in the item's upper right. Doing so removes the item from both your Wall and your News Feed.

Keeping Up-to-Date with Notifications

One of the best arguments for using Facebook on the job is *Notifications*, messages telling you that something involving you happened on the site (page 88). For example, when one of your team members updates a report, you get a Notification; when another one weighs in on a discussion, you get a Notification; and so on. Notifications make your life easier by automating one of the hardest things about keeping projects on track: keeping team members apprised of each others' actions and of project milestones. And you can customize these automated messages to an amazing degree. Here's how to make sure you're notified of just the important stuff:

 Note Facebook doesn't let you *completely* control the Notification process. Stuff you're not interested in is bound to get through occasionally.

1. **Decide which team member activities you want Facebook to share with the group (for example, "Post on a Discussion Board" or "Add a Friend").** To change your settings, at the top right of any Facebook page, click Account, then Privacy Settings. On the page that appears, click the tiny "Customize settings" link and then adjust your settings to control which of your activities your team members get notified about. For example, if you want to make sure all your team members get notified when you post links and photos, click the drop-down menu to the right of the "Posts by me" heading and—assuming you've friended all your team members (page 56)—choose Friends Only.

2. **Tell Facebook which team members you want to keep the closest eye on**. Facebook has the last word on which *stories* (newsy tidbits) appear on the News Feed section of your Home page, but you can influence its selections. To do so: On your Home page (click the Home link at the top of any page to get to it), make sure Top News is selected in the News Feed section. Then scroll down to the bottom of the screen and click the Edit Options link. See page 85 for details on setting story preferences.

3. **Tell Facebook which activities involving *you* you want to be noti-fied about**. Facebook can keep track of just about anything anybody does on the site that involves you. For example, you can tell Facebook to email you when a team member comments on a Note or photo you've posted or tags you in a photo. To adjust your preferences, at the top of any Facebook page, click Account, then Account Settings, and then click the Notifications tab. (See page 90 for more about Notification settings.)

4. **Finally, to ensure consistent Notifications among team members, tell all the members how to adjust *their* settings.**

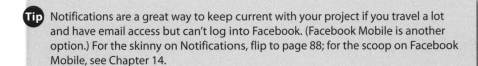

Tip Notifications are a great way to keep current with your project if you travel a lot and have email access but can't log into Facebook. (Facebook Mobile is another option.) For the skinny on Notifications, flip to page 88; for the scoop on Facebook Mobile, see Chapter 14.

Chapter 11
Advertising on Facebook

In Facebook's early days, "advertising" meant college students looking to sell their old textbooks or find new roommates. But now that the site is open to the public and has several hundred million members, things have changed. Facebook's ability to comb through gazillions of personal details at a practically unheard-of level of granularity ("Show me all the single, conservative, male college students who live in Portland and enjoy watching vintage Bugs Bunny reruns") *and* tap directly into each member's circle of friends is an advertiser's dream come true.

These days, big companies with big ad budgets are placing ads on Facebook. As the site has grown, marketing strategies have changed, too, from simple network-targeted banner ads to *social ads*, which mine members' personal details and friend lists to hawk products. This chapter explores your options for advertising on Facebook, which range from free to affordable to don't even think about it.

 Note Facebook recently announced an upcoming feature, Facebook Questions, that will let you ask a question of everyone on the site and—if you like—conduct a poll. To find out more, point your browser to *www.facebook.com/questions*.

Facebook Pages: Profiles for Bands, Brands, and More

The unfortunately named *Pages* (could the Facebook team have possibly come up with a more generic name?) are basically Facebook profiles for things other than people, like TV shows, bands, and companies. Pages combine the detailed info of a personal profile with interactive features and a pretty amazing marketing scheme. And best of all, they're free.

Geared toward freelancers, business owners, musicians, politicians, non-profits, and other small- to large-sized organizations, Pages:

- **Are tailored to meet your needs**. For example, say you set up a band Page (page 176 shows you how). Your Page automatically comes with the standard discussion board, Wall, and photo album features. But wait, there's more: It also includes sections for listing upcoming events and posting video clips, so people can check out your tunes.

- **Aren't subject to a member limit**. Pages can have an unlimited number of fans.

- **Give your organization visibility**. Because people searching Facebook can browse through Pages by clicking the Pages tab in their search results, they're more likely to find your Page than if it was grouped in with a million personal profiles.

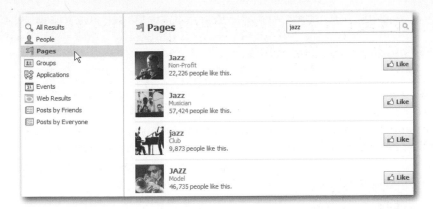

- **Don't cost you anything**. If you want to shoot *social ads* (page 181) to all your Page's fans, you'll need to get out your credit card; but for now, creating a Page is completely free.

How Pages Work

Word of mouth is an effective marketing scheme offline, and it works online, too. When a Facebook member surfs to a Page—by searching, browsing, or following a link he finds on another Facebook member's profile—and likes what he sees, he clicks the Page's thumbs-up "Like" button (see page 180), and then all kinds of interesting things happen:

- **Facebook lists the Page on his profile**. Everyone who visits the Info section of his profile will now see that he's cuckoo for Cocoa Puffs (or likes the band, book, brand, or nonprofit he declared himself a fan of).

- **News of his fan status appears in his friends' News Feeds**.

- **The person or company who created the Page gets to see who's viewing it and how often via *Insights* (page 182), and gets the option of sending news blasts called *updates* (page 180) to all the fans who've declared they like the Page.** For a fee, the Page's creator can also send targeted social ads (page 181) to the fan *and* to everyone on the fan's friend list.

Creating a Page

Here's how to create a free Facebook Page for your business, band, or nonprofit:

> **Tip** *Community Pages* are a subset of regular Pages. Community Pages are for general topics like cooking, movie genres, and cities. When such a Page becomes popular enough, Facebook takes it over and links it to the Wikipedia entry about that topic. If you're a fan of that Community Page (see the next section), you'll start seeing items related to it showing up in your News Feed. Because of that, it's a good idea to only become a fan of Community Pages you're really interested in so your News Feed doesn't fill up with stuff you don't care about.

1. **In the Search field at the top of any Facebook screen, type *pages* and then, in the list of search results that pops up, click Facebook Pages (the one with the blue-and-white F icon).** On the Discover Facebook Pages screen that appears, click the Create Page button, and Facebook displays two forms: one for a Community or fan page, and one for an official, business-oriented page.

> **Tip** Facebook provides a really useful soup-to-nuts guide for creating a Page with pointers on everything from before-you-start marketing strategies ("What will turn your Facebook fans into paying customers?") to practical how-tos and examples. You can find the guide at *www.facebook.com/pages/learn.php*.

2. **On the right side of the page that appears, in the Official Page form, choose a category and name for your Page.** Turning on the "Local business" radio button displays a drop-down list from which you can choose what kind of bricks-and-mortar concern you're hoping to attract attention to: Your options include bar, café, park, store, and lots more. Turn on the "Brand, product, or organization" radio button if you're selling products such as pharmaceuticals or food, or if you're in a business with national reach such as travel or communications. Turning on the "Artist, band, or public figure" radio button gives you freelance options such as writer, politician, and athlete.

After you've picked the appropriate category and given your Page a name, turn on the checkbox next to "I'm the official representative of this person, business, brand, or product and have permission to create this Page" (assuming, of course, that you do). When you finish, click Create Official Page. In the confirmation box that appears, click Create Page.

 Note It's worth clicking the "Review the Facebook Terms" link that appears below the checkbox and taking a couple of minutes to read through exactly what it is you're agreeing to by creating a Facebook page. Some stuff is just common courtesy, like promising not to use your Page to send spam, spread viruses, or con people out of their hard-earned cash. If you're creating a Page for a Facebook application or a website, however, you'll need to abide by a lot more (and a lot more specific) rules, all of which you'll find listed in the terms.

3. **Flesh out your Page**. On the screen that appears, the first thing you want to do is click the "Upload an Image" link to replace the question mark with a picture of your band, your product, or whatever. Next, click the Info tab and then the Edit Information link to build a profile similar to the personal profile you created when you joined Facebook (see page 13) by filling in Basic Info. When you finish building your Page's profile, click the Edit Page link to see a list of all the different applications you can upload tidbits to (such as album info, concert dates, and music clips if you're in a band; to see them all, click the Apps link that appears on the left side of the screen) and settings you can adjust (such as requiring your fans to be over 18; on the left side of the screen, click Manage Permissions).

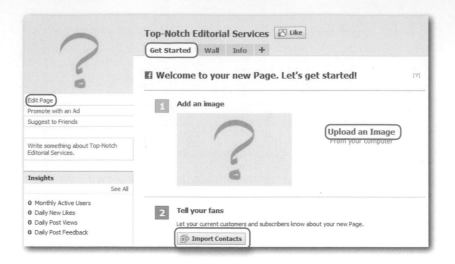

Tip
Clicking the + tab lets you fancy-up your Page with separate tabbed sections for Events, photos, and more. Think video clips of your band, photos of your restaurant, detail-rich Notes for your non-profit—anything that will encourage the folks who visit your Page to learn more about what you can do for them.

4. **Get the word out.** Facebook gives you a couple of ways to let folks know your Page is up and ready for action. One option is to buy a social ad (page 183). Another—good for those who already have a business website up and running—is to add a *widget* or two to your site that whisks website visitors to your Facebook Page (page 189). The quickest and easiest option of all is to send all the folks you know a quick Message letting them know you're open for business on Facebook. To do so: On your Page's Get Started tab, head to the "Tell your fans" section and click the Import Contacts button.

Note
You might not want people peeking at your Page until you're finished adding stuff. If you like, you can pull your Page offline temporarily while you add to it, and then publish it again when it's just the way you want it. To pull it offline: From your Page's profile, click the Edit Page link. Then, on the left side of the page that appears, select Manage Permissions and turn on the checkbox next to Page Visibility. Facebook then displays a "publish this Page" link at the top of your Page's profile that you can click when you're ready to have the world see your handiwork.

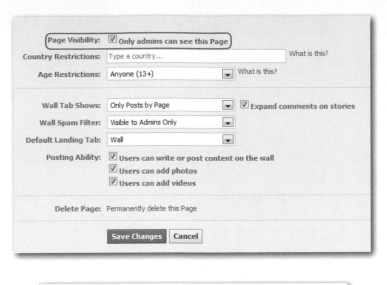

5. **Give people a reason to come back.** Marketing on Facebook isn't so different from marketing in the real world: If you want traffic, you have to remind people you exist on a regular basis. It also couldn't hurt to offer folks fresh reasons to visit your Page and recommend it to their friends once in awhile. (A sale? A new product? An upcoming gig?) To send new info to the News Feeds of your Pages' *fans* (page 180): On the Page's Get Started tab, click the Post Update button (alternatively, click the Wall tab) and then share your tidbit as described on page 78.

 If you expect to post a lot of updates from your mobile phone, you'll want to set up your mobile phone to make the process easy. To do so: On the Page's Get Started tab, scroll down to the "Set up your mobile phone" section and then click either Send Mobile Email (if you expect to upload photos) or Send Text Messages (if all you plan to do is update your Page's status).

6. **Monitor the effectiveness of your Page and tweak it, if necessary.** After you publish your Page, Facebook displays the "Ads and Pages" link in the applications section on the left side of your Home page so you can easily find and change your Page. Facebook also sends you weekly emails letting you know how many folks have visited it lately, how many became fans, and so on. The email contains a "Visit your Insights Page" link to the Insights program (page 182), which displays your weekly numbers in greater detail.

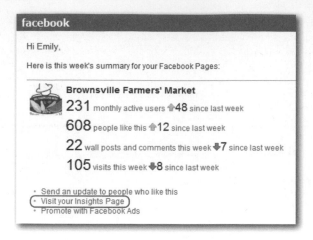

facebook

Hi Emily,

Here is this week's summary for your Facebook Pages:

Brownsville Farmers' Market

231 monthly active users ⬆48 since last week

608 people like this ⬆12 since last week

22 wall posts and comments this week ⬇7 since last week

105 visits this week ⬇8 since last week

• Send an update to people who like this
• Visit your Insights Page
• Promote with Facebook Ads

 Note After you publish a Page, you also receive an occasional Facebook Ads newsletter in your email inbox full of tips and case studies. If you don't think it's useful, you can unsubscribe by clicking the link at the bottom of the newsletter.

Liking Pages

Similar to wearing name-brand clothes and rooting for your favorite sports team, liking a Page (in other words, becoming a fan of it) tells people in your social circle what you're into and what's important to you.

 Tip After you create your own Page, people can locate and declare their liking for it using the steps below. To give your fans even more opportunities to "like" you—and, therefore, more opportunities to put your name in front of *their* friends via their friends' News Feeds—consider adding a Like button to your website (see page 190).

Declaring that you like a Page is easy. Simply find the Page you're interested in (type its name in the Search box, and then click the Pages tab on the search results page), and then click the Like button. (This button appears on the Page itself and on the Page's listing in your search results until you click it; after you become a fan of a Page, the button disappears.) After you click the Like button, Facebook lists the Page in the "Activities and Interests" section on your profile, and news of your newfound fandom appears in your friends' News Feeds.

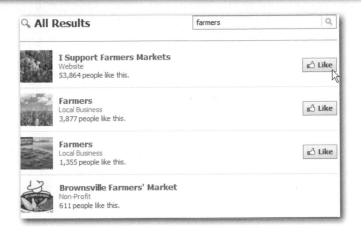

Social Ads (Targeted Announcements)

A *social ad* is an announcement you can broadcast to specific groups of Facebook members, such as men in their 20s, women with college degrees, or married people who work at Wal-Mart and like Beanie Babies. Social ads consist of a graphic and a little text, and they appear either in Facebook's ad space (the right-hand side of each screen), in people's News Feeds (page 84), or both, depending on how much you pay.

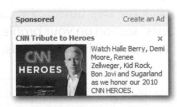

Note If you're new to online marketing (or just want a quick refresher), check out Facebook's marketing primer at *www.facebook.com/adsmarketing*.

Here's how social ads work:

1. **You create an ad and tell Facebook when to run it and which members to target**. Unlike the customized, big-bucks ads you can run if you've got a marketing budget (page 191), creating a social ad is a self-serve proposition, requiring only a few minutes of your time and a credit card. You can get pretty darned specific when it comes to who sees your ad, too. For example, you can have Facebook show it only to single people aged 31 to 36 who have conservative political views and degrees in biology.

 Note Facebook's *social actions* feature an *Open Graph* program (which is basically a new-and-improved version of the old *Connect* program) let you track people who interact with your Facebook Page or application—or with your company's non-Facebook website—and then shoot your ad out to all their friends. The result? An ad that's a little more personal and relevant—and, hopefully, more effective—than average. Keep reading this section for the scoop on social actions, or hop to page 189 for more on Open Graph.

2. **You pay for the ad**. The amount you pay depends on how long you want the ad to run and how many people you want to see it.

3. **Optionally, you can tie your ad to *social actions*, which are the things people do on your Facebook Page or on your company's website**. For example, if you've already created a Page (page 174) or already have a website, you can combine your ad with the "news" headline that someone's friend just became a fan.

4. **Facebook runs your ad**. Depending on factors like how much money you coughed up and how many other ads Facebook has in the hopper, your ad appears either in people's News Feeds or in the space Facebook reserves for ads on the right-hand side of each screen.

5. **You get feedback that helps you assess the ad's effectiveness**. Facebook's *Insights* program generates charts that show you the kind of response your ad is getting (the next section shows an example). If you know how to analyze them (they're pretty straightforward), these charts can help you figure out whether your ad is working or whether you need to tweak it. You get to use Insights for free when you pay for a social ad.

Creating and Running a Social Ad

If you've got a graphic and a couple lines of copy, creating a social ad is nearly as easy as creating a Marketplace ad (page 130). Expect to spend somewhere between $5 and $50 per day, depending on who you want to reach and how long you want your ad to run.

Here's how to create and run a social ad:

1. **Scroll to the bottom of any Facebook screen and click the Advertising link**. Then, on the page that appears, click the green "Create an Ad" button.

2. **Tell Facebook what you want your ad to look like**. In the Design Your Ad section of the "Advertise on Facebook" page, type in the address of the website or Facebook Page you want your ad to drive folks to. Then type in your ad's title (up to 25 characters) and some body copy (up to 135 characters). When you finish, click the Browse button to upload a product photo or logo. Facebook displays your ad-in-progress for you as you build it.

 Note If your image file is bigger than 4 KB or is animated, Facebook won't let you upload it. If the image is larger than 110 × 80 pixels, Facebook will upload it, but will shrink it down to 110 × 80 pixels, so the image will be squished and people won't be able to make out any details. (See the Tip on page 161 to learn how to check an image's file format; the info box that appears also shows your file's size and pixel measurements.)

3. **Tell Facebook who you want to see your ad**. As you select options in the Targeting section, Facebook updates the number on the right side of the screen to give you a rough idea of how many members are in the demographic you've chosen. (Turn on the Male checkbox, for example, and Facebook cuts the figure in half, since about half its members are female.) Click the Show Advanced Targeting Options link if you're interested in targeting folks based on other criteria, such as their level of education or the type of relationship they're in. When you're done, scroll down to the next section.

 Note If you create a social ad *after* you've created a Facebook Page, Event, or application, you can specify that you want to target Facebook members who are fans of your creations or friends of those fans. (You can also tell Facebook *not* to advertise to fans—or fans' friends—of one of your Pages, Events, or applications.) To tweak which fans and friends get to see your ad, in the Targeting section of the "Advertise on Facebook" page, head down to the "Connections on Facebook" label and type something into one of the "Target users who…" fields.

4. **Tell Facebook when you want your ad to run. Use the fields in the Schedule section to specify when (and for how long) you want your ad to run.**

5. **Decide whether you want to accept Facebook's suggested bid price and be done with it, or whether you'd rather set your own bid price.** You don't have to do anything special to accept Facebook's suggested bid price; simply head to step 5 below.

If you'd rather tweak your bid, click the "Set a Different Bid (Advanced Mode)" link. Then, in the new Pricing section that appears, decide what you want your payments to be based on: how many people see your ad but don't necessarily click on it *(pay for impressions)* or how many people the ad actually drives to your site or Page *(pay for clicks)*. Once you make your pick, type in how much you want to pay per 1,000 views (if you chose the "Pay for Impressions" route) or per click (if you chose the "Pay for Clicks" route).

 Note In the marketing biz, the "Pay for Clicks" model is known as CPC ("cost per clicks"), and the "Pay for Impressions" model is known as CPM ("cost per thousand"—M is the roman numeral for 1,000).

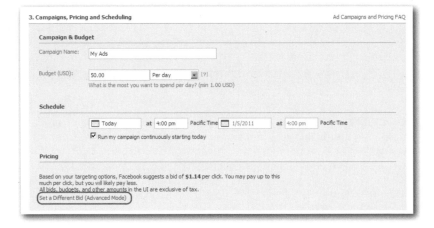

The higher the amount you type in the Max Bid field, the more often your ad appears (in relation to whatever other ads Facebook needs to run the same day as yours; in other words, the highest bidder gets her ads run more often). Because the number of people who log into the site and the total number of ads Facebook sells on any given day fluctuate, you should also double-check the amount listed in the Budget field in the "Campaign & Budget" section. This number indicates the maximum amount you're willing to pay Facebook in any 24-hour period. When you finish, click Review Ad to take one last look at your masterpiece.

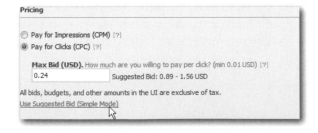

6. **Check your ad for errors and then enter your PayPal or credit card info**. If you spot a mistake, click Edit Ad to go back and fix the error. You should read Facebook's advertising terms and conditions, too. Basically, by running your ad, you certify that you're not lying to people or trying to sell something objectionable or illegal, like drugs, porn, or copyright-protected music. (Just to make sure, your ad won't be published until Facebook approves it, typically an hour or so after you submit it.) Then head to the bottom of the Review Ad page and click the Place Order button.

 Note After you create your ad, you can change it. But if your ad is already running, changing it tells Facebook to stop running it and your ad goes back in the queue to be approved all over again. To change an existing ad, head to the left side of your Home page, click the "Ads and Pages" link, and then click the name of the campaign containing the ad you want to change. On the list of ads that appears, click the name of the one you want to edit. Then click the "edit" link next to the field you want to change or (to tweak the way the ad looks) click the Edit Ad Creative button.

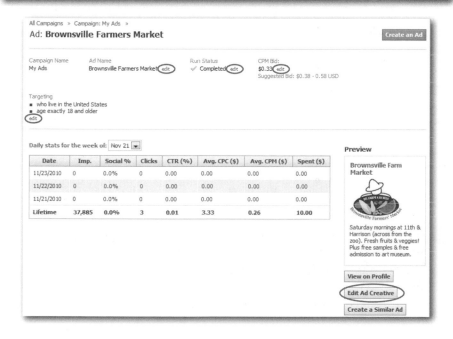

7. **Check on your ad**. You can see daily statistics as well as in-depth demographics (through Facebook's Insights program—see page 182) in as little as a few hours after Facebook starts running your ad. To do so, on the left side of your Home page, click the "Ads and Pages" link and then click the name of the ad campaign you want to check out.

 Tip As you've probably noticed, Facebook updates its site fairly regularly. If a stat appears on your Campaigns page that isn't described below, click the "Ads Manager glossary" link that appears on the left side of the Campaigns page.

Here's a quick rundown of the stats you see:

— **Impressions** tells you how many times the ad has appeared on people's screens.

— **Social %** tells you what percentage of the total impressions appeared on people's screens alongside a social "story" (for example, "Ralph Smith likes Brownsville Farmers Market").

— **Clicks** refers to the number of people who've actually clicked your ad so far.

— **CTR (%)** stands for "click-through rate"; this is the percentage of the people who've seen your ad who've actually clicked it.

— **Avg. CPC ($)** and **Avg. CPM ($)** show you the amount of money you're spending, on average, per click and per thousand impressions, respectively.

— **Spent ($)** keeps track of how much you've spent on the ad so far based on the amount you bid, the number of clicks or impressions your ad has gotten, and how many days your ad has run.

 Note If you bought a long-running ad, you can see day-by-day stats by heading to the menu on the left side of the Campaigns page, clicking Reports, typing in a date range, and then clicking Generate Report.

To dispense with the columns of numbers and see a chart of how your ad is performing, head to the "Choose a graph" drop-down menu and select Clicks, Impressions, or CTR.

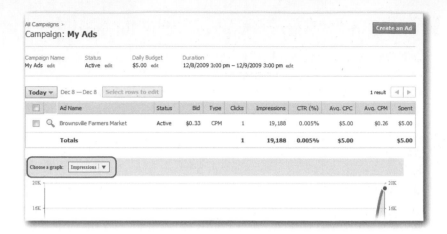

Connect Facebook to Your Website with Widgets

Back in 2007, Facebook debuted a feature called Beacon, which was designed to bring people's Web-surfing actions together with their Facebook friends. A lot of people didn't like Beacon, so Facebook retired it in 2009. They replaced it with a feature called *Connect* and are currently revamping Connect into a new-and-improved feature called *Open Graph*. Using Connect (and, shortly, Open Graph), folks who design applications can create programs that let Facebook members tie their Facebook accounts to certain websites. This is fabulous news if you've got a corporate website, because it lets you tap into your site visitors' activities on other sites—plus their network of Facebook friends—to drive additional traffic to your site and help keep these folks on your site longer, which (theoretically, at least) will lead to better sales. (In marketing speak, Connect and the soon-to-be Open Graph help you *engage* your visitors.)

Connect comes in two flavors:

- **Quick-and-dirty Connect-based programs, a.k.a.** *widgets*, which Facebook divides into *badges* and *social plugins*. These pre-built widgets are so simple to use that even folks with little to no programming experience can add them to their web pages. You'll learn how to add a widget to your web page in a moment.

Rotten Tomatoes Makes Your Facebook Friends Movie Critics

* **Guidelines** (technically, application programming interfaces and specifications) that webmasters and other programmer-types can use to build their own widgets or even more complicated programs for exchanging website visitor info with Facebook info. This option isn't for the average Joe; you want to leave it to programming professionals. For more on this topic, see page 192.

To add a badge widget to your website:

1. **Point your web browser to *www.facebook.com/badges.***

2. **Click the badge you want to add to your site**. Currently, your choices include:

   — **Profile Badge.** After you add it to your blog or website, this widget displays bits of your profile info (such as your profile photo, name, birthday, and email address; you get to choose) in miniature. Clicking on the Profile Badge whisks your blog (or website) visitors to your Facebook profile, where they can find out more about you.

   — **Like Badge.** After you add this widget to your blog or website, it displays a Page Badge (explained in a sec) along with a "[Your Name] likes [Your Page]" message. Clicking on the Like Badge whisks people to your Facebook Page.

Tip Clicking the "Edit this badge" link that appears after you choose a Page or Profile badge and clicking Layout or "Number of Photos" after you choose a Photo Badge allows you to customize what info the badge displays and how the badge looks. You can customize all of the badges except the Like Badge.

— **Photo Badge.** If you add one of these to your blog or website, this widget displays anywhere from 1 to 8 pictures you've previously stored in a Facebook photo album (page 161). Clicking on the Photo Badge takes your site's visitors straight to your photo albums.

— **Page Badge**. After you add a Page Badge, it displays a thumbnail of the Facebook logo over your Facebook Page. Clicking the Badge whisks your site visitors to your Facebook Page, where they can become fans or otherwise interact with your Page.

 Note There are a handful of additional, developer-targeted widgets, called *social plug-ins*, including one that lets your site visitors declare they like your site (and so send news of their newfound fandom to all their friends instantly) and another that lets your site's visitors add comments (and then turn around and share these comments with their Facebook friends). These widgets require a bit more tech-savvy than the Badges, though. You can find a list of them by selecting the "Get our social plugins" link that appears at the bottom of the Facebook Badges Page.

3. **Follow the instructions that appear to add a line or three of HTML code to a page of your website**. Depending on the widget you choose and what kind of website you've got, you may have to cut and paste HTML code directly to your web page's source file. (The process is a bit easier if you're dropping a Page Badge into a blog hosted by Blogger or Typepad.) Don't worry: The widgets were designed to be as simple to add as possible, and Facebook's instructions give you all the details.

High-Dollar Options

Facebook's free and inexpensive Pages, widgets, and social ads are great for small businesses and freelancers. But companies with more dough to throw around can choose from even more advertising options.

 Note If you're looking to drop a serious amount of money on Facebook advertising— thousands of dollars a month, say—you'll want to contact the site directly so you can get special VIP treatment. Head to *www.facebook.com/advertising*, scroll down to the bottom of the page, and then click the Contact Our Sales Team link.

Connect is a customizable feature that does for regular websites what *social actions* (page 182) do for Facebook Pages. It lets you offer your site visitors the option to (what else?) connect with your site, and after they give their go-ahead, their Facebook profiles and friend lists are available for you to use as you wish. For example, if you sell music CDs on your website, you might want to serve up different display ads to the folks whose Facebook profiles mark them as jazz hounds versus the ones whose profiles list classical compositions.

The connection works the other way, too—from your site to Facebook. Not only can you link your site directly to your Facebook Page, you can also incorporate the actions your visitors take on your website into customized "stories" (ads) that Facebook then shoots out to the News Feeds of your site visitors' Facebook friends.

Unless you're talking about one of the simple pre-built widgets described on page 189, adding Connect to your website takes some doing. First, you have to register your site as a Connect application. Then, you either have to use pre-built HTML code snippets (if you're going with one of Facebook's developer widgets) or write your own HTML from scratch based on the Connect guidelines. Facebook doesn't charge for any of these activities, but depending on what you have in mind, you may have to pay your website developers a pretty penny to get the Connect-enabled version of your site up and running. To see what's involved, head to *http://developers.facebook.com/connect.php*.

As mentioned earlier, **Open Graph** is the next generation of Connect. The name and some of the particulars are different, but the goal of both is to connect what goes on in Facebook to what goes on in the rest of the Web. Here's how it works: Say a company's programmers use the Open Graph coding guidelines and application programming interfaces (see below) to attach Like buttons (page 190) to company-sponsored websites, photos, and blog posts. When a Facebook member surfing the Web clicks one of these Like buttons, the company using Open Graph can capture, store, and use that info the same way a Facebook Page does—to display social ads to the person's Facebook friends. The company can also use that information (along with any other info the Facebook member has made publicly available—by choice or accident—*and* any related info any other Open Graph–using company cares to provide) to decide which ads and content to show the member.

For example, say you're bopping around online and you stumble across a cool new designer t-shirt company and a local microbrewery. On both those sites, you click the Like buttons. Then you visit a news site, where you might begin to see ads for ready-to-wear clothing, beer, or both, depending on which other sites you've previously "Liked" and how many times the word "beer" appears on your Facebook profile.

Websites that use Open Graph don't have to use Like buttons in order to access your Facebook info; they can access it behind the scenes, without your having to click a thing. The movie review site *www.rottentomatoes.com*, for example, shows you recommendations based on the movies you've listed on your Facebook profile—and a list of your friends' favorite movies—the very first time you visit the site. (If that creeps you out, you can opt out by heading to the top of the Rotten Tomatoes home page and clicking the Disable or Logout link.)

As this book goes to press, Open Graph is still relatively new, but programmers familiar with Connect should have no trouble switching over to the Open Graph coding guidelines (available at *http://developers.facebook.com/docs/opengraph*) and the related Graph API (*http://developers.facebook.com/docs/api*).

 Facebook's earlier stab at a program to link Facebook to the wider Web, called Beacon, stirred up quite a bit of controversy thanks to the surprise some Facebook members felt when they realized their Web-surfing exploits were being announced to their nearest and dearest Facebook friends—so much controversy, in fact, that Facebook retired Beacon to great fanfare. Interestingly, the new Open Graph hasn't generated anywhere near as much controversy, *even though it works in a similar fashion*, allowing corporate websites to serve up customized ads and content without their site visitors having to give explicit permission allowing websites to tap into and use their Facebook info.

Chapter 12
Customizing Facebook and Adding Apps

Facebook is a pretty polished-looking site, and it wants to stay that way. Unlike MySpace—where you can customize just about everything on your personal page—you can't go hog wild changing the way Facebook looks. You can only adjust the layout of your Home page and profile ever so slightly. But you *can* do something much cooler than, say, changing the background color of your profile page: Facebook lets you add *applications* (a.k.a. apps)—tiny programs that run inside Facebook.

Second only to the friend-to-friend interactions Facebook tracks for you, applications are one of the main reasons for the site's explosive popularity. Why? They're fun! And they can be useful, too. Applications let you do everything from silly stuff (like playing games, "spray painting" on your friends' Walls, or sending your friends virtual potted plants that grow a little each day) to useful things (like creating a terrific-looking resumé right on Facebook). If you can imagine it, somebody's probably created an application that lets you do it.

Facebook granted programmers free access to the Facebook *platform* (the code they need to write things for the site) in May of 2007, meaning that anybody with the programming chops and the desire could create an application. Since then, the number of applications has skyrocketed to over half a *million*, according to Facebook. Read on to learn how to find and install applications.

Modifying Your Home Page and Profile

Facebook gives you a few modest ways to customize the layout of your Home page and profile. You can:

- **Display more menu options on the left side of your Home page**. Simply click the More link at the bottom of the menu. (If you change your mind, click the Less link that appears at the bottom of the new, expanded menu.)

- **Hide news of certain friends' activities**. Your cut-up friend from Biology class just threw another virtual pig at you (it's the 369th, but who's counting?) and your commitment-phobic ex is raving yet again about the diamond ring he just bought—for somebody else. Let's face it: Some news is just plain annoying. To hide news related to a certain friend or Facebook application: On your Home page, head to the right side of any story in your News Feed and click the X that appears. When you do, you're given a chance to tell Facebook whether you want it to quit displaying *all* news about that friend or (if the news has to do with your friend using a Facebook application) that particular application, or to just quit displaying that particular post. Whether you click "Hide this post" or "Hide [friend's or application's name]," the news item disappears.

Tip Facebook remembers which stories you hide and fine-tunes your News Feed accordingly. If you really dig a certain story, click the Like link that appears at the bottom of the story to tell Facebook to display more of that kind of news.

When you tell Facebook to hide a specific post, the site displays a message where the post used to be that says "Post Hidden. This post will no longer appear in your News Feed. Undo". Click the word "Undo" to see the post again.

If you hide all posts from a certain person or application and then have a change of heart and decide you want to see news about him (or it) again, scroll to the bottom of your News Feed and click the Edit Options link. In the dialog box that appears, click either Friends or Applications and then click the "Add to News Feed" link that shows up next to the people and applications, respectively, that you want to see again. When you finish, click Close.

Facebook Applications: An Overview

Facebook *applications* are small programs that run inside Facebook. They're similar to web browser plug-ins (like video players) in that they let you do a little something extra that you couldn't do before you installed them.

 These days, a brand-new application from the Facebook folks called *Places* is getting a lot of attention. Places lets you "check in" with your Facebook friends using a cellphone when you head out to the gym, a coffee shop, a concert, or some other fun-with-pals spot. To use Places, you need to set up your cellphone to work with Facebook. See pages 237 and 245 for details.

If you've had a chance to put Facebook through its paces, you're probably already familiar with the site's built-in applications, which include Notes, Events, and Photos. But people who aren't on the Facebook design team— folks known as "third-party developers"—have written about a bazillion others, such as Music (which lets you add music clips to your profile) and Weekly Schedule (which lets you coordinate a graphic version of your schedule with your coworkers' or friends').

 Because built-in Facebook features including Notes, Links, Photos, and Videos are technically applications, links to them appear in the same section of your Home page as the third-party applications you use.

Most third-party Facebook applications are humorous time-wasters, like the ones that let you spray-paint graffiti on someone's Wall or hurl virtual sheep at your friends in lieu of a sedate poke (page 77). But you may see more serious-minded, business-friendly applications now that Facebook's enormous (and growing) membership is attracting high-dollar advertisers.

Work With Us, for example, is an application that companies looking to hire can use to post jobs, helping you tell at a glance if you have an "in" with a Facebook pal already working there. And Workin' It! offers a list of job openings you can comb through and helps you get word of your job search out to all your Facebook friends.

As you'll learn in this section, Facebook applications are super easy to find, install, and use. Most of them are free, although some (such as games and real-world gift applications) require you to pay using Facebook *credits* (see page 207). The only downsides to using Facebook applications are:

- **An increased risk of exposure to unsavories like phishing scams, malware, and hacked accounts.** Instances of applications misusing member information are rare, but they do exist. Fortunately, Facebook is vigilant about shutting down applications that misbehave.

- **You automatically grant the application's developers access to your profile and, depending on the application, to additional stuff like your friends' profile info and the ability to tell when you're on-line (and when you're not)—all of which poses a security risk.** Flip to page 206 to learn more.

 Tip If you're interested in creating a Facebook application of your own, check out *http://developers.facebook.com* for details on Facebook's development platform. (You can also get to that site by scrolling to the bottom of any Facebook screen and clicking the Developers link.)

Finding Applications

To get a general overview of the kinds of applications that are out there, point your web browser to *www.facebook.com/apps/directory.php*. Alternatively, you can click either the Apps link or—if someone has sent you an invitation to use a specific application—the App Requests link that appears on the left side of your Home page. Then scroll down to the bottom of the screen that appears and click the Apps Directory link.

Facebook displays the All Apps page, which lists a handful of suggested applications at the top. On the left side of the screen, you can click a category (such as Business, Games, or Sports) to see specific kinds of applications. If an application's name piques your interest, click it to find out more.

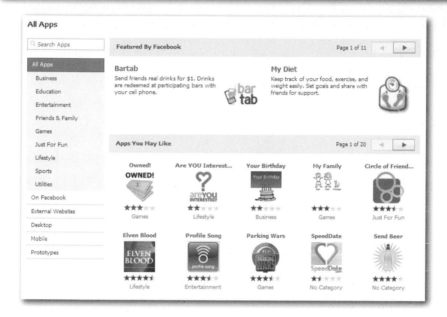

If you're looking for a specific application or type of application, type a word or two into the Search box at the top of any Facebook page and then click the magnifying glass icon. Then, on the left side of the search results page that appears, click the Apps link. Click an application's name or its View App button to learn more about it.

To see what applications your friends are enjoying, head to the left side of your Home page and click either the App Requests link or the Apps link. (If you don't see either of these links, click the More link first.)

No matter which link you click, the Apps page (which Facebook has taken to calling the Applications *dashboard*) that appears is divided into three sections:

- **The applications your friends have invited you to check out** (because, for instance, they want to introduce you to their favorite cause or need another hand at the virtual poker table).

If you clicked the Apps link instead of the Apps Requests link, you don't see this section.

- **The applications you're already using.**
- **The applications (if any) your friends are using.**

 Similar to the old applications "boxes" you used to be able to add to your profile, the Applications dashboard is also where you see any communications from the applications you use. For example, if you choose to play one of the many multi-user Facebook games, your Applications dashboard is where you may be reminded that it's your turn to play.

Adding Applications

You have to install Facebook applications before you can use them, but installing them is a snap. After you find an application as explained in the previous section, click its name to head to its Page and then:

1. **Click the "Go to App" button**.

2. **On the confirmation page that appears, click Allow**. Doing so gives the application access to everything you-related in Facebook (including everything in your profile and the names of the folks you've friended), but if you want to use the application, you don't have any choice—you have to grant it permission to do so.

 If the application is content accessing the information you've already made public (page 219), the confirmation page described in step 2 won't appear.

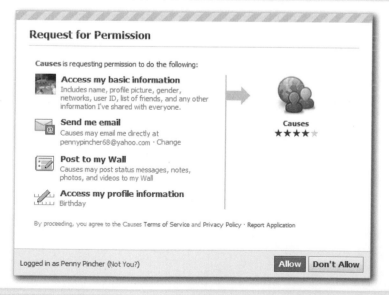

Tip Some applications let you turn off access to certain bits of your Facebook information, although all require you to leave access to most of your info turned on. To see what you can keep private: From any Facebook page, click Account, then choose Privacy Settings. In the "Apps and Websites" section (you may have to scroll down to see it), click the "Edit your settings" link. In the "Apps you use" section of the screen that appears, click the Edit Settings button. Then click the Edit Settings link that appears next to the application in question.

Facebook no longer gives you the option of bookmarking an application so that you can find it again easily the next time you want to use it. The site *may* decide to bookmark an application for you (based on stuff like how often you use the application), but you have no control over that. If Facebook does bookmark an application for you, you'll find it listed on the left side of your Home page. If it doesn't, you can find the application by following the steps on page 203.

 To un-bookmark an application, find the application's link on the left side of your Home page (you may have to click the More link to see it) and then click the X that appears to the left of the application's name when you hover your cursor over it.

Using Applications

The way you use an application and the things you can do with it depend on the application itself. There are also a variety of ways to open an application so you can use it. The most reliable route is to head to the top of your screen and click Account, then choose Privacy Settings. In the "Apps and Websites" section, click the "Edit your settings" link. In the "Apps you use" section of the screen that appears, click the Edit Settings button. On the screen that appears, click the name of the application you want to launch and, finally—in the upper-left corner of the application description area that appears—click the name of the application once again. When you do, Facebook whisks you to the application's main page.

There are also a few other possibilities: If Facebook decided to bookmark an application as explained in the previous section, you can click its name on the left side of your Home page to open it. And if your friends use an application, you'll see it listed in their status updates from time to time. Wherever you find an application's link, as soon as you click it, Facebook displays the application, all ready to go.

Troubleshooting Applications

If an application doesn't behave the way you expect it to, you've got a couple of options: delete it (see page 205) or check to see if it has a Help or Frequently Asked Questions page. If there's no Help page, or if the FAQ doesn't answer your question, you can contact the folks who created the application. Here's how to check for a Help page and contact an application's creator:

1. **At the top of any Facebook screen, click Account and then Help Center**. Alternatively, scroll to the bottom of any Facebook screen and click the Help Center link.

2. **On the left-hand side of the Help Center, click "Games and Apps"**.

3. **In the "Apps by External Developers" list, click the name of the application you need help with**.

4. **On the Help page that appears, read through the suggestions**.

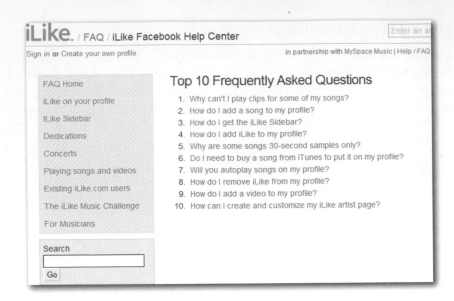

Tip If the application doesn't have a Help page, or if you read the Help page and it doesn't help, you've got one more option: At the top right of any Facebook screen, click Account and then click Help Center. In the "Facebook Apps and Features" section, click the App Support link, then "Bugs and Known Issues on Facebook Platform". The list that appears may give you some insight into the cause of your application woes; if not, head back to the application and see if you can track down a contact email address. (If the application's problem is that it won't display properly, try searching for its Page in the Facebook Search box, as described on page 174.)

Controlling Who Knows You're Using Applications

When you add and start using a Facebook application, Facebook assumes you want all your friends to know you're using it, and typically posts info about your application-related activities on your Wall and to your friend's News Feeds.

But maybe you use Facebook at the office and don't want your fellow cube-dwellers to know you're spending your coffee breaks playing Farmville. Or maybe you like to maintain a cool, worldly image and would rather not let your fellow hipsters know about your weakness for Cute Catz. Whatever your reasons, you can tell Facebook whether or not you want the site to announce what you do with an application on your Wall and in your friends' News Feeds.

To change who gets to know you're using an application:

1. **At the top right of any Facebook page, click Account and then Privacy Settings**.

2. **On the Choose Your Privacy Settings page that appears, scroll down to the "Apps and Websites" section and click the "Edit your settings" link.**

3. **On the page that appears, click the drop-down box next to "Game and app activity" and make your selection.**

Deleting Applications

If you decide you don't like an application or never remember to use it (and would prefer that it not continue to collect personal information about you and your friends), you can delete it quickly and easily:

1. **At the top right of any Facebook page, click Account and then Privacy Settings**.

2. **On the Choose Your Privacy Settings page that appears, scroll down to the "Apps and Websites" section and click the "Edit your settings" link.**

3. **In the "Apps you use" section of the page that appears, click the word "Remove" (it has a red X next to it).**

4. **On the Apps You Use page, find the name of the application you want to delete and click the X that appears to the right of its name**.

5. **In the confirmation box, click Remove**.

If you change your mind and want to use the application again, simply reinstall it (page 201).

 Tip To hide an application without deleting it, click the X that appears next to its name on the left side of your Home page. (To un-hide it, click the See Hidden link that appears on the left side of your Home page.)

Applications and Privacy

Before you can install an application, you have to agree to give that application's creators access to all—yes, *all*—the personal info you've typed into Facebook (that's what the "Request for Permission" box is about—see page 134). What's more, you may also be granting the application's creators access to all of the personal info your *friends* typed into Facebook. Facebook isn't responsible if the application's creators use your personal data (or your friends') for nefarious purposes, lose it, sell it, or write it across the sky in 200-foot-high letters. That's a scary thought—especially if you or your friends have added home address, credit card info, or other super-sensitive details to your Facebook accounts.

Chapter 13 discusses privacy in detail, and you really, really ought to read it. But the gist is this: When deciding whether you want to share your info, think about how much sensitive stuff you've typed into Facebook, how bad off you'd be if it fell into the wrong hands, and how useful you find the application you want to install.

Facebook Games

Technically, games on Facebook are nothing more than regular applications—ones designed to help you have fun with your friends, that is. (Admit it: Who doesn't like to take a break from work now and then to play a hand of cards or virtual cops-and-robbers?)

Games are by far the most popular applications on Facebook. By Facebook's estimates, 40% of all members regularly use the site to play games, which—at the time of this writing—translates to somewhere around 200 million people. And while there are dozens of Facebook games to choose from, the top handful are breathtakingly popular, each boasting around

10 million regular players. Some folks even join Facebook just *because* of the games. The upshot? Facebook has amped up its support for game developers—as well as game players—by instituting a way to pay for special game-related extras, such as virtual poker chips in the popular Texas HoldEm Poker game (see below). And rumors are circulating about a specialized gaming portal (a one-stop website devoted to all things game-related) in Facebook's future.

 Note Facebook members are polarized when it comes to so-called *social games* (games you play online that—like most games you play in the real world—involve other people): Almost as many people hate them as love them. If you're one of the former, you may want to take a quick peek at the section on Facebook *credits* (see below), which can be useful for purchasing stuff like birthday gifts and charitable donations using non-game applications—and then skip ahead to the next chapter.

Facebook games are different from other applications in two important ways:

- **Facebook gives you a special way to find new games and store your favorites.** You can find games the same way you find other applications (page 198); just click the Games link on the search results page instead of the Apps link. But Facebook gives you an even easier way to find and organize games: It displays a Games link on your Home page. Check out page 208 for details.

- **Some games let you use Facebook credits.** Facebook *credits* are virtual currency you can use to pay for premiums or "extras" in some Facebook games—things like fancy game pieces and additional levels. Here's how it works: You use your credit card to buy a wad of Facebook credits (currently the exchange rate is ten cents per credit). Then, when you're playing a game and want to buy, say, a souped-up virtual tractor, you tell the application to transfer the cost of one virtual tractor from your Facebook credit account (rather than having to whip out your credit card all over again).

The following sections explain how to install games and use credits.

 Tip Games currently popular on Facebook include card games (such as Texas HoldEm Poker), virtual world–type games (like FarmVille and FrontierVille), and role-playing games (such as Mafia Wars). And chances are that if you enjoy a popular television or board game (such as Wheel of Fortune or Scrabble), a Facebook version either exists or soon will. To see which games made the latest Top 10 list, head to one of the many social network and gaming watch-sites, such as *www.insidefacebook.com* or *www.insidesocialgames.com*.

Finding Games

Facebook makes finding games easy:

1. **On the left side of your Home page, click the Games link.** If you've been on Facebook long enough to receive a game invitation from a pal, you'll see the Games Requests link instead of the Games link.

2. **On the Games page (technically called the Games *dashboard*) that appears, browse the games directory by category and click the name of the game you want to play.** If your friends have sent you any game invitations, you'll see them here—along with lists of all the games your friends are playing—instead of the games directory.

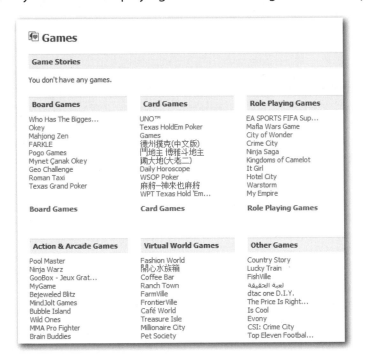

 If your Games dashboard is stuffed with requests to play games from your pals, you won't see the handy games directory. To find new games, you need to head to the Applications directory (at the bottom of the Games dashboard, click the Games Directory link or check out page 198).

 Tip By default, your friends will see news of the games you play in their News Feeds. To keep this from happening (seriously, do you want the fact that you play Frogger to get out?) you need to adjust your application privacy settings. Page 220 shows you how.

Paying for Games (and Other Stuff) with Facebook Credits

As you learned earlier, Facebook credits are a form of Facebook-only currency you can spend on Facebook applications and games. For example, you can buy virtual birthday cards (from the Hallmark Social Calendar application, say) and virtual game tokens (such as special crop seeds in the game FarmVille), as well as make donations (through the Stand Up to Cancer application, for instance).

Here's how it works. You transfer real-world money to your Facebook credits account using your credit card, PayPal, or cellphone. After you have a credits account balance, you can use your credits whenever you like to buy stuff from Facebook applications and games. Though relatively new, Facebook credits are already expected to generate *$1 billion* in sales this year, and are currently accepted by over 200 different Facebook games and applications.

 Note To see an up-to-date list of all the applications, including games, that accept Facebook credits, head to Facebook's Help Center (page 253), search for the word "games", and then click the "What games and applications can I use Facebook Credits with?" link that appears.

Buying Credits

If you've got a credit card, a PayPal account, or a cellphone, you can buy Facebook credits. The current exchange rate is around $0.10–0.15 per credit depending on how you pay and how many you purchase.

 Note Facebook credits aren't available in every country. Currently, in the U.S., large retailers including Walmart, Safeway, and Target sell Facebook-credit gift cards in $10 and $25 denominations.

To buy Facebook credits:

1. **At the top of any screen, click Account, then Credits Balance.**

 Note If you don't see the Credits Balance link when you click Account, click the Account Settings link instead. Then, on the My Account page that appears, click the Payments tab.

2. **On the Payments tab that appears, click the "buy more" link.**

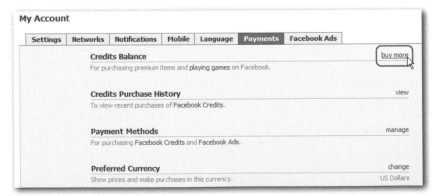

3. **In the Get Facebook Credits box, choose how you want to pay, and then click Continue.** Click the "Show more payment options" link if you have a gift card you want to redeem.

 Facebook lets you earn credits by doing stuff for its partners—for example, filling out surveys, getting approved for a loan, or making a purchase. For details, in the Get Facebook Credits box, turn on the "Earn for free by shopping" radio button.

4. **In the updated box that appears, tell Facebook how many credits you want to buy.** When you finish, click Continue (or, if Facebook already has your payment info, click Buy Now).

5. **In the new window that appears, type in the info Facebook requests and, when you finish, click Complete Purchase**. The details (and the name of the click-to-buy button) you see in this window depend on the payment option you chose in step 3. After you click Complete Purchase—or the alternate click-to-buy button Facebook presents you with—Facebook sends you a Notification and you see a confirmation box confirming your purchase.

Checking Your Credits Balance

You may want to check your credits balance right after you buy something with them, just to double-check that your purchase went through. Or, if you haven't spent any of your credits recently, you can check to refresh your memory about how many you have burning a hole in your virtual pocket.

To check your credits balance: At the top of any Facebook screen page, click Accounts, then Credits Balance. The number of credits available for you to spend is listed on the Payments tab below the "buy more" link.

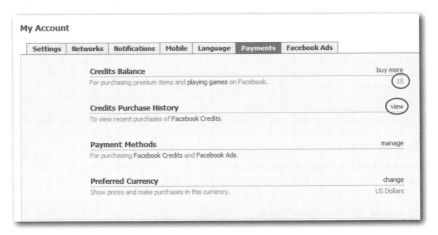

 If the credit balance Facebook displays doesn't match the balance you thought you had, click the "view" link that appears to the right of the Credits Purchase History label and then click View Receipt. Doing so shows you purchase details, including when you bought the credits and how you paid.

Using Credits

Every game and application is different, but the main idea behind paying for stuff with Facebook credits is the same no matter which one you're using: At some point, the game (or other application) asks if you want to buy something or make a donation, and if you say yes, you're given a payment option or three—one of which is to use your Facebook credits.

After you make a purchase using credits, Facebook automatically deducts the correct number of credits from your account.

Chapter 13
Playing It Safe: Facebook Privacy

Social networking sites like Facebook depend on millions of people voluntarily divulging accurate personal information. But in a world where identity theft is a growing concern and spammers can't wait to get their hands on your email address, how do you take advantage of what Facebook has to offer while minimizing risks to your personal info? This chapter explains Facebook's privacy issues and gives you strategies for staying safe—from up-front planning to adjusting your privacy settings to after-the-fact damage control.

Privacy and Facebook: An Overview

If you're connected to the Internet, you should be concerned about your privacy. Surf the Web—privacy risk. Use email—privacy risk. The sad truth is that there are a lot of bad guys out there, and your personal info is worth a lot of money to some of them. Even virus-protection programs and firewalls can't always keep bad things from happening to you. And while Facebook promises to do all it can to protect the personal data you add to your profile, mistakes happen.

 Note To read Facebook's privacy policy, point your web browser to *www.facebook.com/policy.php*.

If you're like most people, your personal info is already stored in lots of databases (your bank's, your favorite magazine's, and so on). But what's unique about Facebook's cache of personal data is that it includes intimate details (like your views on politics, religion, and relationships) that are tied to a *picture* of you (your profile picture), and that it links you to other people—all of whom have also divulged mountains of intimate details—and that it tracks your activities online. This combination of identifying details, an image, and a detailed map of your social habits is what makes Facebook so interesting and compelling—but also so potentially dangerous. Theoretically, someone could find out what town you live in , where you plan to be next Tuesday at 8:00 p.m. (a book club meeting you RSVP'd to on Facebook, for example), and that you're involved with a lot of charities. Armed with your picture, that someone could show up at your book club and try to convince you he's your long-lost cousin Al who's down on his luck and needs a couple thousand bucks to tide him over.

The trick is to balance the benefits you get from using Facebook (and the Internet in general) with the risk of losing control of your private information.

Privacy Threats

Some of the privacy threats associated with Facebook are the same that many online companies face, such as reports that the Facebook source code (the raw programming info that powers the site) was once leaked onto the Internet, potentially giving hackers access to Facebook members' personal data. And, of course, any info you send via the Internet is vulnerable to interception. But there are other Facebook-specific threats, too:

- **Third-party application developers and other Facebook partners**. As explained in Chapter 12, before you can use a Facebook application, you have to grant the person or company who created it access to your personal data as well as—in many cases—the personal data of all your friends. Once you grant that access, control of your (and your friends') personal info is out of Facebook's hands: If the application's creator misuses your information, the beef is between you and them. Likewise, Facebook's privacy policy lets the site share your personal details with companies who advertise or sell products on Facebook, and it's up to those firms to keep your data safe.

- **People you didn't think had access to your profile**. If you think only people who live in your city, attended your alma mater, or work at your company can view your profile, you're mistaken. Hiring managers, parents, teachers, police officers, and other folks who are determined to view your Facebook profile can find a way to do so—either by asking a coworker or friend who happens to be a member of your Facebook network to look up your info or (in the case of cops) by getting a court order.

- **Anybody using a search engine**. Depending on your Facebook privacy settings, *anybody* can search your profile information using a garden-variety search engine such as Yahoo or Google, even if he's not a Facebook member.

 Note Because many of Facebook's privacy settings are opt out (meaning Facebook assumes you want the whole world to see your personal info until you tell it differently), your info is at risk until you adjust your settings as explained in this chapter.

Strategies for Keeping Your Info Private

So that's the bad news. The *good* news is that just three simple strategies give you quite a bit of control over keeping your private data safe:

- **Don't put sensitive info on Facebook**. You get to choose what kind of information you share with the site, and how much. Data thieves can't steal your Social Security number, for example, if you don't make it available.

- **Customize your privacy settings**. Much as keeping your front door locked dramatically reduces the chance of being robbed, customizing your privacy settings minimizes—but doesn't *eliminate*—the chance of your Facebook data falling into the wrong hands. This chapter shows you which settings can help protect your privacy.

- **If the worst happens, fight back**. If a spurned lover tracks you down on Facebook and starts harassing you, you can shut her down by blocking her access to your Facebook profile (page 231) or reporting her to the site (page 232).

Deciding How Much to Share

How confessional you want to be when you create your Facebook profile is entirely up to you. But here are a few things to consider:

- **Give Facebook only enough info to get what you want out of the site**. If you're looking to connect with other early-music fans, for example, limit your profile info to medieval subjects. And if you plan to use Facebook to find parenting tips, you don't need to share your academic and professional background.

- **Consider keeping your public and private identities separate**. If you're planning to use Facebook primarily for networking, think twice about posting pictures of your wild weekend in Jamaica. You don't have to forego mentions of your personal life completely, but you should limit your personal info to the kind of thing you'd feel comfortable tacking up on your cubicle wall.

- **Think about creating an email address just for Facebook**. Companies such as Google and Yahoo let you create a free, Web-based email address you can use to sign up for Facebook. Using an email address dedicated to Facebook protects your "real" work or home email address from accidental or deliberate theft (think spammers).

- **If it's sensitive and optional, leave it out**. Random people viewing your profile don't need to know your home address or phone number. If you meet people on Facebook and want to share this info with them, you can always do so in a more private way (such as a Facebook Message—page 70).

- **When in doubt, do the mom-or-boss check**. If you'd be comfortable telling your mom or your boss something, go ahead and post it on your profile. Otherwise, skip it.

 Note Facebook doesn't care how much info you put in your profile, but it does demand that what you share is accurate and truthful. Creating a "Fakebook"—an account with a bogus name and made-up profile details—can get you banned from the site.

Controlling Access to Your Account

While you need to be wary of people getting access to your account info online, don't forget to take precautions in the real world, too: Make sure no one can log into Facebook as you.

You already know not to share your password with anyone, but there are a couple more steps you should take to protect your account. To prevent co-workers, fellow students, or family members from using your computer to access your Facebook account (either by accident or design), follow these steps:

1. **Log in the smart way**. After you type your email address and Facebook password into the login page (*www.facebook.com/login.php*), make sure the "Keep me logged in" checkbox is turned off before you click the Login button.

2. **Log out when you're finished using Facebook**. Before you go on to the next item on your to-do list, take a second to click the Logout link found in the Account drop-down menu in the upper-right corner of every Facebook screen. Doing so prevents people from getting into your account.

Adjusting Your Privacy Settings

Facebook does a lot of media chest-thumping about how strictly it protects its members' privacy. So it may come as a surprise that, unless you change them, *many privacy settings are set to the slackest possible levels*. It's up to you to understand how Facebook's privacy settings work, where to find them, how to adjust them—and to actually spend time battening down the hatches. That's a lot of work! Fortunately, this book has done most of the work for you; all you have to do is read this section and adjust your settings.

Facebook organizes its privacy settings into three broad, slightly confusing categories:

- **Connecting on Facebook.** The settings in this category let you control the "big chunks" of your profile—the stuff Facebook encourages (but doesn't require) you to let all your fellow Facebook members see, so that old friends and colleagues will be able to get in touch with you. This is where you decide who gets to see where you work, where you go (or went) to school, where you live, and what kinds of stuff you like to do in your spare time. It's also where you tell the site who gets to search for you in Facebook and who gets to send you Messages (perfect strangers or only the folks in your networks, for example).

- **Sharing on Facebook.** These settings let you tell Facebook who gets to see the rest of your profile, including your photos and contact info. This category also lets you control who gets to see stuff other people do on Facebook that pertains to you, such as commenting on your posts and tagging you in photos.

- **Apps and Websites.** The settings in this category let you decide who gets to know about the applications (including games) you use, as well as what information about you *and your friends* those applications get to access. Head to this category to control whether or not folks without Facebook accounts can see your Facebook profile info using a search engine such as Yahoo or Google.

 Tip It might seem like a lot of hassle to plod through each category, but it won't take you more than a few minutes, especially with this chapter to guide you. And it's time well spent: You really, *really* ought to know who's doing what with your (and your friends') private information.

Controlling Who Sees Your Profile, Contact, and Friend Info

You need to comb through a couple screens of settings to control who sees what about you. Here's how:

1. **At the top right of any Facebook screen, click the Account link and then, in the drop-down list that appears, click Privacy Settings.**

2. **On the Choose Your Privacy Settings screen that appears, tweak the settings in the three main categories:**

— **Connecting on Facebook.** To access these settings, click the View Settings link below the "Connecting on Facebook" heading. As mentioned in the previous section, this is where you tell Facebook who you want to be able to search for you on Facebook, send you friend requests and Messages, and access part of your profile page.

There are only a handful of settings on this page, and the options are pretty much the same. If, for example, you want to let long-lost friends and coworkers look you up based on the interests and activities you typed into the Personal Information section of your profile, head to the drop-down list next to "See your likes, activities and other connections" and either keep the Everyone setting that Facebook starts you out with, or select "Friends of Friends" to let anyone who's friends with any of your friends see that info. Choosing Friends Only keeps Facebook members who aren't on your friend list from seeing your profile, and choosing Customize lets you type in specific folks you want to have (or *not* have) access to the information in this particular section of your profile.

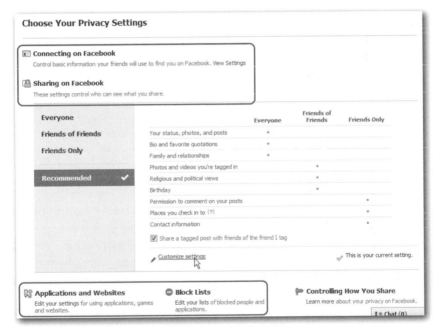

 Note Alas, you can no longer grant (or deny) access to a *list* of folks, such as a list of fellow students, bowling-team buddies, or coworkers.

Choose Your Privacy Settings ▸ Connecting on Facebook

‹ Back to Privacy   Preview My Profile

Your name, profile picture, gender and networks are visible to everyone (learn more). We also recommend setting the other basic settings below open to everyone so friends can find and connect with you.

🔍 **Search for you on Facebook**	This lets friends and family find you in Facebook search results. Set this to Everyone or you could miss friend requests.	🔒 Everyone ▾
👥 **Send you friend requests**	This lets you receive friend requests. Set this to Everyone to avoid missing out on chances to connect with people you know.	🔒 Everyone ▾
💬 **Send you messages**	This helps you make sure you know people before adding them as friends.	🔒 Everyone ▾
👥 **See your friend list**	This lets you connect with people based on friends you have in common. Your friend list is always available to applications and your connections to friends may be visible elsewhere.	🔒 Everyone ▾
💼 **See your education and work**	This helps you connect with classmates and colleagues, and discover new professional opportunities.	🔒 Everyone ▾
🏙 **See your current city and hometown**	This helps you get in touch with neighbors and old friends. Note: you can separately control how you share places you check in to on the main privacy page.	🔒 Everyone ▾
✏ **See your likes, activities and other connections**	This lets you express your interests and experiences, and connect with people who like the same things you do.	🔒 Everyone ▾

 Note Because it can be hard to remember what your profile looks like to other people when you're in the middle of privacy-tweaking, Facebook gives you a way to double-check: On the "Choose Your Privacy Settings—Connecting on Facebook" page, click the Preview My Profile button to take a peek at what someone who falls in the Everyone category will see when he runs across your profile listing on Facebook. (If you want to see what a *particular* Facebook member—like your boss, say—can see based on your current settings, on the preview profile page, click in the "Start typing a friend's name" box, type in that person's name, and then hit Enter.)

—   **Sharing on Facebook**. To tweak these settings, on the Choose Your Privacy Settings page, head to the bottom of the "Sharing on Facebook" section (the big table that takes up most of the screen) and click the tiny "Customize settings" link. The settings on the page that appears let you control who gets to see the bits of your profile not covered in the "Connecting on Facebook" category—things like your religious and political views, birthday, and the places you check into (this last is only useful if you use the Places application via your cellphone; see page 245 for details). This is also where you control who gets to comment on the stuff you share with your pals, such as Wall posts and photos, and who gets to view non-Facebook ways to contact you, like your phone number, address, and instant messaging screen name.

Adjust all these settings to Only Friends unless you have a darn good reason not to (if, for example, you signed up with Facebook because you're coordinating your high school reunion and want far-flung former classmates to be able to contact you). And consider choosing the Customize setting and then, in the Custom Privacy box that appears, selecting Only Me from the "These people" menu for any email addresses that you've given Facebook. That'll prevent folks you don't know from clogging your personal or work email account with spam.

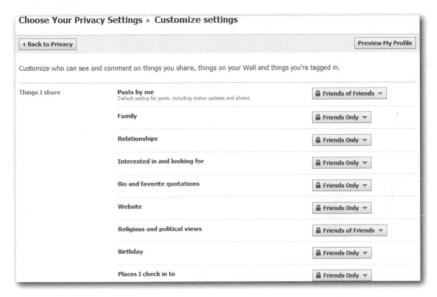

 The "Sharing on Facebook" section also lets you choose who sees your personal website (if you have one); in most cases, you'll want to select the Everyone option for this setting.

— **Apps and Websites.** This section is where you specify how much of your profile information you want the applications you use, the applications your *friends* use, and the Facebook-enabled websites you visit (page 193) to have access to. This section also gives you a chance to keep news of your latest favorite application from hitting your friends' News Feeds. (Not everybody needs to know that you've logged the 10,000 hours required to become expert in Bay City Rollers Trivia, for example.) Flip to page 205 for details.

3. **If necessary, add people to your Block Lists**. Considering the enormous number of people using the site, the incidents of Facebook stalking and other unsavory behaviors are actually pretty low. Still, it's nice to know that if someone *does* cross the line from mildly annoying to upsetting, heading to this section and clicking the "Edit your lists" link gives you an easy way to remove him from your Facebook life. Page 231 has the details.

 Tip Alternatively, you can block a friend *or* a non-friend by heading to the left side of her profile and clicking the "Report/Block this Person" link (you may have to scroll down to see it).

Hiding from Facebook and Web Searches

Unless you tell it not to, Facebook shows your name and profile picture to everyone who looks you up using Facebook's search feature (page 48)—and lets them message and befriend you—as well as to any non-Facebook member who looks you up using a search engine such as Google. Big deal, right? Letting folks find you and contact you is the reason most people join Facebook, after all.

Actually, it *is* a big deal. If someone who doesn't ordinarily get to see your profile info pokes you, for example, or sends you a Facebook message and you respond to it, *Facebook automatically grants that person temporary access to your profile.*

 Note Blocking someone (page 231) prevents them from seeing your profile or interacting with you on Facebook in any way.

If the thought of unintentionally granting profile access to people you don't know makes you a little nervous, you've got three choices:

- **Tell Facebook not to display your name or picture in non-friends' search results**. This is a good choice if you're not interested in long-lost friends or potential employers looking you up, but instead joined Facebook to keep in touch with people you already know. To choose this option: At the top right of any Facebook page, click the Account link and then click Privacy Settings. On the Privacy Settings page that appears, in the "Connecting on Facebook" section, click the "View Settings" link. On the page that appears, head to the "Search for you on Facebook" section and, from the drop-down list, choose Friends Only.

Choose Your Privacy Settings ▸ Connecting on Facebook

| ◂ Back to Privacy | Previe |

Your name, profile picture, gender and networks are visible to everyone (learn more). We also recommend setting the c settings below open to everyone so friends can find and connect with you.

🔍 **Search for you on Facebook** — This lets friends and family find you in Facebook search results. Set this to Everyone or you could miss friend requests.   🔒 **Friends Only** ▾

Tip To keep people (including non-Facebook members) from looking you up on Facebook using an Internet search engine, see page 225.

- **Customize how non-friend Facebook members who aren't in your networks can contact you**. Choose this option if you want to let people look you up out of the blue, but don't want Messages from folks you don't know (yet) clogging up your Facebook inbox. Here's how: At the top of any Facebook page, click the Account link, and then click Privacy Settings. On the Privacy Settings page that appears, click the "View Settings" link in the "Connecting on Facebook" section. On the page that appears, scroll down to the "Send you friend requests" and "Send you messages" settings. Then choose which group of folks you want to be able to look for you on Facebook and then send you friend requests and Messages straight from their search results.

- **Hide your Facebook account from non-Facebook search engines.** Unless you tell it otherwise, Facebook assumes you want your profile listing—that tiny one-line-and-a-picture search result that lets folks scouring Facebook know you're a member—to be visible to any other Facebook member. It also assumes you want all the info you've made visible to everyone on Facebook to be visible to everyone on the *Internet*. If that's not what you want: At the top of any Facebook page, click the Account link, and then click Privacy Settings. On the Privacy Settings page that appears, in the "Apps and Websites" section, click the "Edit your settings" link. Then scroll down to the "Public search" section and click the Edit Settings button there. On the page that appears, turn off the "Enable public search" checkbox to keep search engines like Yahoo from accessing your profile info.

Deciding What Applications Can Access (and Blab)

As you learned in the last chapter, you can't use a third-party Facebook application without granting the application access to your profile information. And if you're friends with someone who has installed a Facebook application, *that* application has access to your profile info, too—unless you adjust your privacy settings.

 Tip You can cut down on—but not eliminate—the *social ads* (page 181) about you that Facebook displays on your friends' Home and profile pages. To do so: At the top of any Facebook page, click the Account link and then click Account Settings. On the page that appears, click the Facebook Ads tab. Then, from the "Allow ads on platform pages to show my information to" drop-down list, choose "No one", and then click the Save Changes button that appears just below drop-down list. Finally, scroll down to the "Show my social actions in Facebook Ads to" drop-down list, choose "No one", and then click the Save Changes button that appears just below *that* drop-down list.

To limit the amount of your profile information that your friends' applications can access:

1. **At the top right of any Facebook page, click the Account link and then click Privacy Settings**.

2. **On the Choose Your Privacy Settings page that appears, scroll down to the "Apps and Websites" section and click the "Edit your settings" link.** Facebook revamped its privacy settings recently, so now you've got quite a bit of control over what parts of your profile applications can mine.

Here are your choices:

— **Apps you use**. Clicking the name of an application displays a page that shows you what profile info the application has access to. Depending on the application, you may be able to turn off some of that access (in which case you see a blue Remove link next to a specific bit of information). Or you may be stuck with just two choices: Letting the application access your profile willy-nilly, or removing that application altogether (in which case the label Required appears next to all bits of info the application is accessing).

Click the Edit Settings link to the right of any application's name to see any tweaks you can make to the application's ability to access your profile. Click the "Remove app" link to pull the application's access to your data altogether.

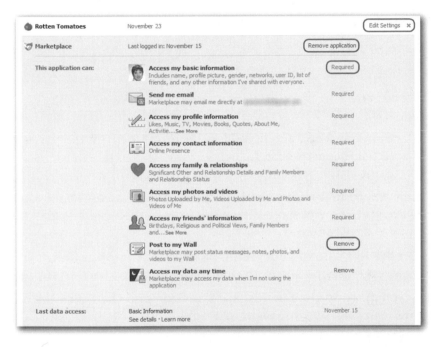

— **Info accessible through your friends**. Say your friends are all playing the latest Facebook game. Click the Edit Settings button to the right of the "Info accessible through your friends" heading to display a dialog box that lets you control what that game gets to know about *you* (even if you've never played it before in your life and have no intention of doing so).

Info accessible through your friends

Use the settings below to control which of your information is available to applications, games and websites when your friends use them. The more info you share, the more social the experience.

☐ Bio	☐ My videos
☐ Birthday	☐ My links
☐ Family and relationships	☐ My notes
☐ Interested in and looking for	☐ Photos and videos I'm tagged in
☐ Religious and political views	☐ Hometown
☑ My website	☐ Current city
☐ If I'm online	☐ Education and work
☐ My status updates	☐ Activities, interests, things I like
☐ My photos	☑ Places I check in to

Your name, profile picture, gender, networks and user ID (along with any other information you've set to everyone) is available to friends' applications unless you turn off platform applications and websites.

Save Changes   Cancel

— **Game and app activity**. Click this drop-down list (see page 205) to tell Facebook who, if anyone, you want to receive news of the games and applications you use.

Another way to limit what your friends' applications can see about you is to *block* applications, which prevents them from getting *any* info about you. To block an application:

1. **On the left side of your Home page, click the Apps link**. If you've been on Facebook awhile, the link might read App Requests instead.

2. **Scroll down to the Friends' Apps section and then click the name of the application you want to block**.

3. **On the left side of the "Request for Permission" box that appears (page 134), click the application's name**.

4. **On the application's page that appears, click the Block App link**.

Tip To see a list of all your blocked applications, at the top right of any Facebook page, click the Account link and then click Privacy Settings. Next, scroll down to the Block Lists section and click the "Edit your lists" link. Then scroll down to the bottom of the page that appears to see the list of all the apps you've blocked. These applications can't access any info about you or contact you, but they may still appear on your friends' profiles. If you want to unblock an application, click the "Unblock" link next to its name.

Controlling Which Sites Can Access Your Profile

Facebook's partnerships with other companies through its Connect and brand-new Open Graph programs (page 189) let non-Facebook websites use your Facebook profile info—and vice versa. For example, a website might use your Facebook profile info (combined with your friends' profile info and data about your friends' recent website purchases) to display a list of recommendations right there on the website, like "Your friend Pat loves the latest Terminator movie! Click here to buy it!". Alternatively, an Open Graph or Connect-enabled site may help you post bits of its content to your Facebook Wall (by displaying a "Post to your Facebook Wall" link pre-filled with site information) or shoot out custom ads to your Facebook friends based on what you did on the site ("Fred just bought high-top tennis shoes from our site. Want a pair?").

When you interact with one of Facebook's Open Graph- or Connect-enabled partners by surfing to its website, the site may do one of several things:

- **It may automatically access your Facebook profile info and display customized content based on that information while giving you the option to opt out.**

- **It may do nothing *until* you click a button with a Facebook icon on it—such as a Login, Share, Connect with Facebook, or Like button—at which point it may:**

    — Ask for permission to access your info.

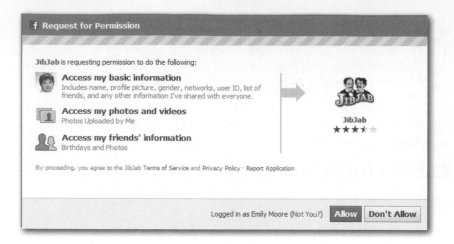

Note The exact wording of the link you see—as well as the wording of the explanation, if any—depends on the way the site chooses to use Connect and Open Graph.

— Pop up a box that lets you post site info (in other words, an ad for the site) to your Wall or send it directly to your friends.

— Automatically shoot news of your newfound fandom to your friends' News Feeds.

You have three options when it comes to controlling how external websites can access your profile info:

- **If the site displays a Facebook icon, you can opt not to click the icon.** Alternatively, you can click the icon and follow any instructions that appear.

- **If the site displays a message asking for permission to access your profile info, you can grant (or deny) permission.**

- **If you granted a website permission to access your Facebook info (or can't remember whether you did or not), you can retract your permission.** To do so:

  1. At the top of any Facebook page, click the Account link and then click Privacy Settings.

  2. On the Choose Your Privacy Settings page that appears, scroll down to the "Apps and Websites" section and click the "Edit your settings" link.

  3. Scroll down to the "Instant personalization" section and click the Edit Settings button.

  4. On the page that appears, turn off the "Enable instant personalization on partner websites" checkbox.

Fighting Back

If you're being harassed by another Facebook member—someone fills your Wall with unsavory comments, for example, sends you threatening messages, or pokes you 50 times a day—you can take action. The first thing you want to do is stop your tormentor from contacting you on Facebook. If that doesn't do the trick, you can take self-defense a step further and report the person to Facebook. This section teaches you how.

Blocking Individual Members

Facebook lets you prevent individual members from knowing that you're even on the site. *Blocking* someone keeps him from seeing your profile, finding you with Facebook searches, or contacting you via Facebook. To block someone:

1. **At the top of any Facebook page, click the Account link and then click Privacy Settings**.

Note To prevent people who aren't on Facebook from using a search engine like Google to see that you're on Facebook, you have to tell Facebook *not* to create a public search listing for you. Page 225 explains how to do that.

2. **On the Privacy Settings page that appears, scroll down to the Block Lists section and click the "Edit your lists" link.**

3. **In the Name field of the page that appears, type the name of the member you want to block and then click the Block This User button.**

 Note If the person who's been bugging you is a shady character and you happen to know the email address he likely used when he registered for Facebook—but not the Facebook alias he's using this week—type in his email address instead of his name and then click Block This User.

4. **In the search results that appear, find the person you want to block and click the Block link next to his name.**

 Note You can also block someone by going to their Facebook profile page and clicking the Report/Block this Person link on the left side of the page (you may have to scroll down to see it). This same link lets you report a violation by this person (see the next section).

Reporting Violations

Facebook takes violations of its privacy policy seriously. It makes reporting potential violations easy by displaying a Report link on every Facebook application's page and next to virtually every potentially offensive bit of info members add to the site, from discussion threads to Wall posts.

 Note "Offensive" can mean anything from pornographic to threatening. To see a list of what Facebook considers offensive, check out the Safety section of the site's "Statement of Rights and Responsibilities:" *www.facebook.com/terms.php*.

In addition to getting upset by things other members post on Walls or upload to their profiles, people sometimes find third-party applications offensive. Examples of potentially offensive applications include those that revolve around a tasteless pastime (seeing how many nude photos you can upload, say), those that don't work (or work differently than advertised), or those you suspect of misusing your profile info.

To report an application:

1. **On the left side of your Home page, click the Applications (or Application Requests) link.**

2. **In the list that appears, find the application you want to report and then click its name.**

3. **On the application page that appears, click the "Report/Contact this Application" link on the bottom left side of the screen.**

4. **In the pop-up window Facebook displays, use the drop-down list to tell Facebook why you're reporting the application.** Type your comments into the text field, and then click the Submit button.

> **Tip** To report offensive content, send an email to *abuse@facebook.com*.

> **Note** To learn more ways to keep your info safe—including strategies for protecting your kids as they venture onto Facebook—scroll to the top of any Facebook screen, click the Account link and then click Help Center. On the left side of the page that appears, click the Safety link.

Chapter 14
Facebook Mobile

F acebook can be addictive. If you're away from a computer and feel the need to check in on your Facebook friends, update your status, or upload that photo you just took with your cellphone (nearly half of all Facebook members do), you can use *Facebook Mobile* on your cellphone to stay in the loop. If you like, you can even use your cellphone (along with a new Facebook application called *Places*) to "check in" to your favorite haunts—cafés, bookstores, restaurants, and so on—so that you can easily meet up with your online friends in real life. Whether you travel a lot or just like to stay connected when you're between work and home, Facebook Mobile is a handy way to keep up with your Facebook friends without a computer.

How Facebook Mobile Works

Facebook Mobile is an application (see Chapter 12) that lets you use your Internet-ready cellphone to:

- **Interact with Facebook on your phone's teeny-tiny screen**. Facebook's *Mobile Web* feature (page 240) lets you use the browser on your cellphone to see a scaled-down version of the Facebook website. Using your phone's keypad, you can do things like update your status, find out what your friends are doing, look up people's phone numbers, and keep tabs on the Events you've signed up for.

Tip If you own a BlackBerry, an iPhone, or another popular "smartphone," there's likely a specially designed Facebook application you can use to access Facebook *directly* from your phone (rather than a scaled-down version of the site). To see if there's a special application for your phone, point your phone's web browser to *www.face-book.com/mobile* and scroll down to the "Facebook for your phone" section.

- **Interact with Facebook via text messages**. The *Mobile Texts* feature (page 241) lets you interact with Facebook from your phone *without* having to go through the mobile version of the Facebook website. (This option is usually faster than the Mobile Web feature, and is the way to go if your phone doesn't have a web browser; you do, of course, need a phone that lets you send text messages.) If you want to write a quickie message on a friend's Wall, for example, you can text-message a specific Facebook code (see page 242) along with your friend's name and your message. You can also sign up to receive texts when you get a friend request or when your friends change their status, post on your Wall, or send you a Facebook Message.

- **Upload photos and video clips**. Perfect for posting impromptu additions to Groups and Events (as well as for tracking project updates), Facebook's *Mobile Uploads* feature (page 243) lets you sling the media clips you capture with your phone directly to your Facebook account.

- **Subscribe to your friends' status updates**. You can choose to receive a text message every time one of your Facebook friends updates his Facebook status—useful for keeping your finger on the pulse of close friendships (or team members) when you're away from your computer.

Like all Facebook applications, Facebook Mobile is free to use. But don't forget that every time you use it, you're likely racking up charges on your cellphone bill. If your phone company charges you every time you use your phone to connect to the Web or send a text message, that means you pay every time you access the Facebook site or poke a Facebook friend via text message.

 Note Facebook Mobile is great for quickie tasks like looking up profile info, checking Event start times, and announcing your status. It's *not* so great for text-intensive tasks you occasionally do on Facebook, such as fleshing out your profile or writing a 12-page Note.

Setting Up Facebook Mobile

Before you can use Facebook Mobile, you have to do a little bit of easy setup. You just need to activate your phone number and then adjust your mobile settings. The following sections show you how.

 Note Although Facebook Mobile is a Facebook application, you don't install it the way you do other applications. Instead, you have to follow the activation process explained in the next section.

Activating Your Phone

Activating your phone means associating a cellphone number with your Facebook account, and then testing the connection between your phone and Facebook. To activate your phone:

1. **At the top right of any Facebook screen, click the Account link and then, in the drop-down list that appears, click Account Settings**. On the Account Settings page, click the Mobile tab.

2. **On the Mobile tab, click the "Register for Facebook Text Messages" link.**

3. **In the "Step 1 of 2" box that appears, select your country and cell-phone company from the drop-down lists, and then click Next**. Facebook Mobile works with most cellphone companies, but if yours isn't listed, you're out of luck.

4. **In the "Step 2 of 2" box, follow the instructions to send Facebook a message from your cellphone.**

5. **Check your cellphone**. It may take a few minutes for the text message with your confirmation code to arrive. If you don't get a text from Facebook after 15 minutes or so, send Facebook a text message one more time, making sure you follow the onscreen instructions carefully.

Tip If you surfed away from the "Step 2 of 2" box while you were waiting for your confirmation code, no sweat: Just click the "Already receive a mobile confirmation code?" link that appears on the Mobile tab.

6. **Type your confirmation code into the "Step 2 of 2" box's text field, turn off the "Add this phone number to my profile" checkbox if you don't want all your Facebook friends to have your cell number, and then click Next**. After you do, Facebook sends a confirmation text message to your phone and, on your computer, displays a successful activation message across the top of a page you can use to edit your mobile settings. You can now start interacting with Facebook using your cellphone, though it's a good idea to edit your mobile settings before you get started; see the next section for details.

> **Confirmed!**
> Facebook Text Messages are now activated. Text 32665 (FBOOK) to update your status. You can also receive texts when people poke, message, wall post, or friend you. Learn more about Facebook Text Messages

Adjusting Your Settings

You'll want to adjust your Facebook Mobile settings right after you activate your phone because they affect the type, number, and timing of text messages you receive from Facebook. (You may not appreciate getting poked at 3:00 a.m. by your cut-up, night-owl friend Bob, for example.)

To customize your mobile settings:

1. **Head to the Facebook Mobile page**. As explained in the previous section, Facebook automatically displays this page after you finish activating your phone. But if you surfed away from that page, at the top right of any Facebook page, click the Account link and choose Account Settings; then click the Mobile tab.

2. **On the Mobile tab, use the checkboxes, radio buttons, and drop-down lists to tell Facebook what kinds of text messages you want to receive**. When you finish, click Save Preferences.

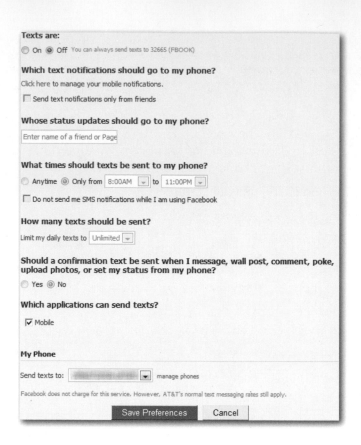

Texts are:

○ On ◉ Off You can always send texts to 32665 (FBOOK)

Which text notifications should go to my phone?

Click here to manage your mobile notifications.

☐ Send text notifications only from friends

Whose status updates should go to my phone?

Enter name of a friend or Page

What times should texts be sent to my phone?

○ Anytime ◉ Only from 8:00AM ▾ to 11:00PM ▾

☐ Do not send me SMS notifications while I am using Facebook

How many texts should be sent?

Limit my daily texts to Unlimited ▾

Should a confirmation text be sent when I message, wall post, comment, poke, upload photos, or set my status from my phone?

○ Yes ◉ No

Which applications can send texts?

☑ Mobile

My Phone

Send texts to: ▓▓▓▓▓▓▓▓▓▓ ▾ manage phones

Facebook does not charge for this service. However, AT&T's normal text messaging rates still apply.

[Save Preferences]   [Cancel]

 Tip You can set up more than one cellphone to work with your Facebook account. To do so, scroll to the bottom of the Mobile tab and click the tiny "manage phones" link. In the Mobile Phones section of the revised Mobile tab that Facebook displays, click the "Add another phone" link. Then follow the activation process explained on page 237.

Using Facebook Mobile

After you've activated at least one cellphone *and* tweaked your mobile settings, you're ready to use Facebook Mobile. The following sections show you how.

Surfing Facebook from Your Phone

To view and interact with a scaled-down version of Facebook specially designed for cellphones, point your cellphone's web browser to *http://m.facebook.com* and log in with your regular Facebook login and password. (Exactly how you get to the site depends on the cellphone you're using; check your phone's manual for instructions.)

If you own an iPhone, head to the iPhone-optimized version of Facebook at *http:// iphone.facebook.com* instead.

You can do almost as much on the mobile version of Facebook as you can on the regular version. The kinds of things you probably want to do (and that are easiest to do using the hunt-and-peck method most people employ when using phones as personal computers) include:

- Viewing and changing your status
- Checking the status of your friends
- Searching for people
- Tracking your upcoming events
- Uploading photos and videos (assuming your phone can take photos and videos)
- Viewing your friends' photos and videos
- Checking into and out of places (but only if you use the Places application; see page 245 for details)
- Viewing your News Feed

Interacting with Facebook via Text Message

You can do many of the quick, basic things you do on Facebook—like updating your status or sending someone a Message—more easily by sending a short text message from your cellphone than by using your phone's screen to browse and interact with the Facebook Mobile website.

 To have Facebook send *you* a text message when someone adds you as a friend, sends you a message on Facebook, tags you in a photo, or does something else pertaining to you: On your computer, head to the top right of any Facebook screen and click Account, then Account Settings. In the My Account page that appears, click the Notifications tab and then turn on the SMS checkbox next to any action you want to be notified of via text. (To get texted when a friend changes his status, see page 92.)

To text message Facebook, send a message to 32665 (that's FBOOK for folks who prefer looking at the letters on the keypad rather than the numbers). Table 14-1 shows you the different things you can do by text-messaging 32665. If what you want to text has something to do with another Facebook member, make sure you type in the person's full name. (And depending on how common that name is, you might have to jockey with your cellphone a bit to make sure you reach the right person; see the Note at the bottom of this page.)

Table 1-1. Actions you can take by text-messaging 32665 (FBOOK)

Action	Code	Text message example
Update your status*		at a Halloween party
Delete your last status update	Undo	**undo**
Search for somebody's profile info	search	**search** john doe
Get somebody's cell number	cell	**cell** john doe
Send somebody a Message	msg	**msg** john doe how did the interview go?
Poke somebody	poke	**poke** john doe
Post on somebody's Wall	wall	**wall** john doe congrats on the new gig
Send a friend request to somebody	add	**add** john doe
Write a Note	note	**note** having a great time in vegas
Get help on how to text Facebook	help	**help**

*You don't need to type any special code to update your status; simply type the message you want to appear on your profile

 Note Texting Facebook isn't instantaneous: It can take anywhere from a few minutes to a few hours for your actions to be reflected on the site. When they are, Facebook text messages you to let you know (if you've told it to; see page 90).

Facebook has set up a spiffy, interactive page where you can practice sending texts to the site. Check it out at *www.facebook.com/mobile/?texts=1*.

 Note If there happens to be more than one Facebook member named John Doe (and there almost always is), Facebook text messages you back with a list of people you can choose from to make sure your message reaches the John Doe in Springfield who graduated from Stanford in '88. Simply choose from the list and shoot your message back to Facebook.

Uploading a Picture or Video

If you've got a cellphone that snaps pictures or shoots video, you can upload your photos or video clips straight to Facebook. Here's how:

1. **Get a special upload email from Facebook**. At the top right of any Facebook screen, click the Account link and then choose Account settings. On the My Account screen that appears, click the Mobile tab and then click the "Go to Facebook Mobile" link in the upper-right part of the screen. Then jot down your special upload email address listed in the "Upload via Email" section (or, alternatively, click "Send my upload email to me now" to save your upload email address in your regular email inbox).

Upload via Email

Use a personalized upload email to post status updates or send photos and videos straight to your profile. Your personal email is:

~~~~~~~~~~~~~~~~~~~~~~

Send my upload email to me now

Find out more

2. **Send some pictures or video clips**. After you complete step 1 above, you're good to go: You can send pictures to your special upload email address willy-nilly. (Exactly *how* you send email from your cellphone depends on the phone; check the manual for instructions.) In the subject line of your message, type a caption for your picture or video; in the body of your message, type in a description.

Subscribing to Friends' Status Updates

Say you're out of town and you've got a sick friend you want to keep tabs on. You can have Facebook text you your friend's status each time she updates it. To do so:

1. **At the top of any Facebook page, click the Account link, then choose Account Settings.**

2. **On the My Account page that appears, click the mobile tab, and scroll down to the "Whose status updates should go to my phone?" section.** (You'll only see this section if you've activated at least one cellphone—see page 237.)

3. **Start typing a friend's name into the "Enter name of a friend" field.** As you type, Facebook displays a list of matching names; click the one you want. Then, in the box that pops up, click Confirm.

That's it! You're subscribed. The next time your friend updates her status, you'll get a text message containing the new status. If you decide you want to unsubscribe

from someone's updates, head to the Mobile tab's "Whose status updates should go to my phone?" section again and click tiny the "remove" link that appears next to the name of the friend whose status you no longer want sent to your phone.

Deactivating Your Phone

If you change your cellphone number or just change your mind about using Facebook Mobile, you can turn off the service quickly and easily.

 Note You don't have to wait until you get back to your computer to deactivate your cellphone; you can do it right from your phone using the Facebook Mobile site. Either way, simply follow the steps below.

1. **At the top right of any Facebook screen, click Account and then Account Settings.**

2. **On the My Account page that appears, click the Mobile tab.**

3. **Near the top of the Mobile tab, find the phone number you want to deactivate and then click the "remove" link next to it.** In the confirmation box that pops up, click the Remove Phone button.

 Note Sometimes cellphone numbers get reassigned, and nothing's more aggravating than receiving text messages you don't want (but that you may end up paying for). To stop receiving messages from Facebook, send a text message to 32665 (that's FBOOK) that includes the word "stop" or "off."

Checking In with Places

If you live in the United States and your cellphone is a relatively new model that can run HTML 5 and has GPS (like an iPhone, for example), you can use Facebook's new *Places* application to "check into" places like bars and coffee shops. (Facebook plans to make Places available in other countries soon.) Why would you want to check into a place? Because doing so:

- **Announces your location on your Facebook friends' News Feeds** and lets you see which, if any, of your Places-using friends happen to be in the neighborhood—upping the chance of a serendipitous get-together.

 Thanks to a deal Facebook struck with other popular GPS-based services including Yelp and Gowalla, when you use Places you get to see folks who've checked in using those services, too.

- **Lets you read what other folks have to say about the place**—like "Definitely order the Mississippi Mud Cake, it's to die for"—and post your own review.

- **Gives you details such as maps, directions, and the names of other folks checked into other, similar places nearby** (just in case reading some of the reviews of your first choice made you want to jump ship).

- **May result in loot,** as some restaurants, stores, and museums offer real-world goodies—such as discounts and other deals—to folks who check in with Places.

 When you use Places, you automatically give Facebook ultra-personal information without actually having to type it in—and not just your current whereabouts, either. You also divulge stuff like which friends you care enough about to hang out with in person, which stores and restaurants you frequent, and even (should you spring for a few of those Facebook-check-in deals some places offer) your buying habits. Maybe you don't mind Facebook having all this info. But keep in mind that the non-Facebook applications you *or* any of your friends use may be privy to it, too (see page 220). Page 247 shows you how to take advantage of Places while minimizing the risk.

Getting Set Up

Currently, to get the most out of Places, you need to have one of the following:

- **An iPhone to which you've downloaded the "Facebook for iPhone" app (see below).** Before you can use Places, you also need to tell your iPhone it's okay for Facebook to locate you using your phone's built-in global positioning system (page 247).

- **An Android cellphone that has the "Facebook for Android" app on it.** Most Android phones come with this app built in. If yours didn't, you can find out where and how to download the application by searching Facebook's Applications directory (page 198) for "Facebook for Android".

The following sections give step-by-step instructions for using Places on an iPhone, but the steps are almost exactly the same on Android phones.

 Facebook is hoping to have Places working on Blackberry phones in the very near future. Until then, if you don't have an iPhone or an Android, you can point the touch-, browser-, and geolocation-enabled cellphone you *do* have to *http://touch. facebook.com*. Tap the Places tab that appears in the upper right of the screen, and—when prompted—tap "Share location" to check in. The screens you see should be similar to the ones described below. (Unfortunately, at the time of this writing, the check-in deals are only good if you're using an iPhone running the "Facebook for iPhone" application.)

To download "Facebook for iPhone":

1. **On your iPhone, click the App Store icon.**

2. **Tap the Search icon, type in *Facebook*, and tap the Search button.**

3. **In the search results, tap the Facebook icon that appears.**

4. **On the Info page for the Facebook app, tap the word "Free", and then tap Install.**

5. **Type in your Facebook password and (if necessary) verify your credit card information.** When you finish, tap Buy. You know you've successfully downloaded the app when the Facebook logo appears on your iPhone.

After you download "iPhone for Facebook", you need to tell your iPhone to let Facebook locate you using your phone's built-in GPS.

 Until you do the following steps, Places may *appear* to work on your iPhone—until you try to check in, at which point it displays the "Locating…" message indefinitely.

1. **On your iPhone's main screen, tap the Settings icon.**
2. **On the Settings screen, tap General.**
3. **Tap Location Services.**
4. **Tap the On/Off button next to Facebook so that it displays ON.**

Adjusting Your Privacy Settings

Privacy on Facebook is a pretty huge deal, which is why Chapter 13 is devoted to the subject. But privacy takes on a whole new level of importance when it concerns your real-world comings and goings—which is exactly what using Places is all about. So before you start checking into places all over your city, you want to make sure you tell Facebook who gets to know about those places.

 The steps below work whether you're using your computer or your cellphone.

To adjust your Places-related privacy settings:

1. **In the top right of any Facebook screen, click Account, then Privacy Settings.** If you're on an iPhone, launch the Facebook app and then head to the upper-left part of the screen and tap Account, then Privacy Settings. (If you don't see the word "Account", tap the square in the upper-left part of the screen to get to your home screen.)
2. **Scroll to the bottom of the "Sharing on Facebook" section and click (or tap) the tiny "Customize settings" link.**
3. **Click (or tap) the drop-down box next to "Places I check in to" to tell Facebook who gets to see where you are.** All of your friends? All of your friends except, say, your boss? It's up to you.

4. **Make sure the checkbox next to "Include me in 'People Here Now' after I check in" is turned off**—unless you want your Facebook friends *and* people in the neighborhood to know who you are. Most of the time, announcing your proximity to perfect strangers isn't such a hot idea. But you may want to turn on the checkbox if, for example, you've breezed into town for a convention, agreed to meet a group of coworkers for dinner, and headed to what you only *thought* was the right restaurant but don't see anyone you know.

5. **Decide whether you want to let your friends announce where you are.** Scroll down and click (or tap) the Edit Settings button next to "Friends can check me in to Places." Then, in the "Places: Friend Tags" box that appears, choose Enabled from the Select One drop-down list if, say, you're headed to a club with a bunch of pals and forgot to bring along your cellphone. Otherwise, choose Disabled.

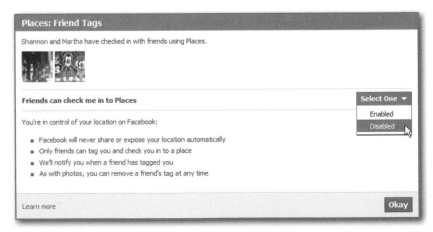

6. **Decide whether you want the applications your *friends* use to know and store Places-related info about you, including where you are, who you're there with, and what you buy.** On the Choose Your Privacy Settings screen (from any Facebook screen, click or tap Account, then Privacy Settings), scroll down to the "Apps and Web-sites" section and click (or tap) the "Edit your settings" link. Next, click (or tap) the Edit Settings button in the "Info accessible through your friends" section and then turn off the checkbox next to "Places I check in to" to hide your location (and other Places-related info) from your friends' applications and games.

Checking Yourself (and Your Friends) In

To check into a restaurant, bar, museum, library, or any other place:

1. **On your iPhone, launch the Facebook app.** A bunch of icons appear, including the Places icon, which looks like a red pin on a map. (If you don't see this icon, tap the square in the upper-left part of the screen.)

2. **Tap Places.** A list of check-ins appears—both yours (if you recently check into a place) and your friends'.

3. **In the upper right of the screen that appears, tap Check In.**

4. **On the Nearby Places screen that appears, either tap the name of a place or—if the spot you happen to be at isn't listed—tap the "Find or Add a Place" field to type in the name of the restaurant (or other place) you want to check into.**

Tip If you tap a place and notice something isn't quite right—the phone number or address is wrong, for example, or you know for a fact the place has been boarded up for months—you can tell Facebook so they can look into it. To do so: Tap the right-pointing arrow that appears in the upper-right corner of the "[Name of place]" screen.

5. **After you find (or type in) the place you want to check into, check yourself (and, optionally, your pals) in.** You can type a quick one-liner in the "What are you doing?" field, if you like. If you're accompanied by a few friends, you can check them in too by tapping the Tag Friends With You link. When you're ready to check yourself in, tap Check In.

Note *Tagging* a friend and *checking him in* are the same thing—for now. When Places first debuted, there *was* a difference between the two, although the difference was mighty confusing. Here's how it used to work: If you checked yourself into a place and tagged your friend Barney, all your friends got to see that Barney was there with you (even if he had adjusted his settings to tell Facebook nobody else could check him in). If Barney had told Facebook his friends *could* check him in, then tagging him resulted in, well, checking him in—meaning that his friends *and* your friends (and anyone else viewing the place's Page) would see news of his where-abouts. Perhaps because of the privacy concerns this hard-to-figure-out feature stirred up, Facebook changed things so that turning off your friends' ability to check you in (page 248) now *also* keeps them from tagging you. Because Places is still in its infancy, however, don't be surprised if the way you check in and tag your friends changes.

When you check in somewhere, a few things happen:

— On the Place's Facebook page, your profile picture appears in the Here Now list (unless you told Facebook differently; see page 248). If any of your Facebook friends are currently checked into the same spot, you see them listed, too.

— If you tagged a friend who has never used Places before, she sees a confirmation box when she logs into Facebook asking if it's okay for you to check her in. If she says yes, she'll receive a Notification letting her know that you did, indeed, check her in, and where (depending on how she tweaked her privacy settings; see page 74).

— Depending on how you and your friend adjusted your respective privacy settings, news of your (and your friend's) whereabouts appear in your (and her) News Feeds, accompanied by a Places icon.

You can only check in pals if they haven't turned off the ability for other people to do so (see page 248, step 5).

 The rules regarding who gets to see your current location are different for under-age Facebook members. If you registered on Facebook as being under 18, only your friends get to see details of the places you check into.

Finding Your Friends

To find out where your friends are hanging out:

1. **On your iPhone, launch the Facebook app.** The Places icon appears surrounded by several other icons. (If you don't see these icons, click the square in the upper-right part of the screen.)

2. **Tap Places.** A list of check-ins appears—both yours (if you recently checked into a place) and your friends'.

3. **Tap the friend you're interested in.** On the Comments screen that appears, you can either tap the "Write a comment…" field to leave a message ("You planning to be there for another hour? I'm right across the street.") or tap the name of the place and then tap Info at the bottom of the screen to get a map and directions. To see all the folks checked into a place (along with any comments or reviews they've typed in), tap the name of the place and then tap Activity.

 Checking into a place automatically shows you a list of Facebook friends who checked into that same place.

Removing a Check-in

Facebook doesn't actually give you a way to check *out* of places. Your check-ins stay on your News Feed, buried—over time—by newer stuff, including your subsequent check-ins. If you like, however, you can delete a check-in. This is useful if, for example, you checked into the wrong place by mistake, or one of your cut-up friends checked you into a mental hospital (virtually, of course) for a yuk before you figured out how to keep him from doing it (see step 5 on page 248).

To remove a check-in using your computer:

1. **On your profile page or News Feed, mouse over the check-in story you want to remove.**

2. **Click the X that appears on the right side of the story.**

 You can also delete a check-in using your cellphone. To remove a check-in from an iPhone: Head to your profile or News Feed, and then swipe left or right over the check-in story and tap the Delete button that appears.

Appendix
Getting Help

acebook is pretty easy to use—especially if you keep this book handy. But Facebook's design team regularly adds new features and changes existing ones. So, someday soon you may log into Facebook and find a new menu option or discover that your favorite application doesn't work the way it used to. When that happens, you can get up to speed quickly by checking Facebook's Help section or getting info from other websites that cover Facebook. Read on to learn more.

> **Tip** Don't want to type these website addresses by hand? No problem! Head to *www. missingmanuals.com/cds* and click the Missing CD-ROM link next to this book's cover. Voilà—a clickable, chapter-by-chapter list of all the websites mentioned in these pages.

Facebook Help

Unlike some online help pages, Facebook Help is easy to find, well-written, succinct—and usually helpful (imagine that). To access Facebook Help:

1. **Head to the top right of any Facebook screen and click Account; then, from the drop-down list that appears, choose Help Center**.

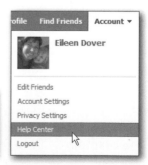

> **Note** Clicking the Help link that appears at the bottom right of every Facebook screen also sends you directly to the Facebook Help Center.

2. **On the Help Center screen that appears, click the topic you want to know more about**. You can also type a phrase into the "What can we help you with?" field and then hit Enter.

 Tip Two of the links on the left side of the Help Center screen are especially useful: Getting Started and Safety. Clicking them whisks you to useful articles studded with how-to links.

3. **If the Help topic you picked doesn't answer your question, click a different one (or type a different phrase into the "What can we help you with?" field)**. If you just can't find what you're looking for, you can contact Facebook and ask for help, as explained on page 256.

Note To alert you to features that have changed recently or that are temporarily misbehaving, Facebook displays known site glitches in big, pink boxes at the top of the Help Center screen.

Getting Help from Other Facebook Members

In any community, you find a certain percentage of kindhearted, knowledgeable folks willing to take a few minutes to share their expertise and help you on your way—and Facebook is no different. Because the site's sheer number of members pretty much precludes you from getting a quick response from Facebook's technical gurus, your best shot at getting speedy help with puzzling Facebook questions is to ask other members.

To post a question on one of Facebook's Help forums:

1. **Scroll to the bottom right of any Facebook screen and click the Help link**.

2. **On the left side of the Help Center screen that appears, click Help Discussions**.

3. **On the Help Discussion Topics screen, click the topic that's vexing you**.

4. **In the list of topic-related items that appears, click the issue that most closely matches yours**.

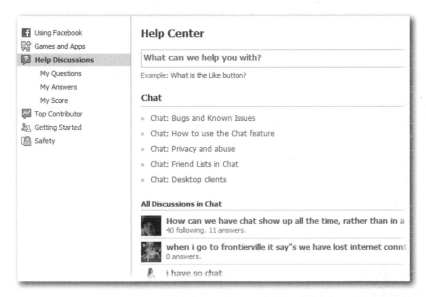

5. **Take a look at the questions other members have asked (and answered)**. If you still need help, click the New Question button to ask a question. Facebook's notification process (page 88) will alert you when someone answers your question.

Contacting Facebook

The downside to being as popular as Facebook is that the personal touch can get lost in the shuffle. A few years ago, for example, every Help screen gave members the opportunity to send a complaint, suggestion, or attaboy directly to Facebook's technical staff. These days, click-here-to-contact-us links are as rare as hen's teeth.

The one place these contact-us links most often appear is at the bottom of some (thought not all) Help screens. To contact Facebook:

1. **Head to the bottom of any screen and click the Help link**.

2. **On the Help Center screen that appears, click the Suggestions icon (it looks like a tiny wooden suggestions box with a card sticking out of the top)**. If you don't see the Suggestions link, mouse over to the left side of the screen and make sure the Using Facebook link is selected.

3. **On the "Suggestions and Feedback" page that appears, click the topic most related to your request, comment, or gripe**. If no topic comes close to what you want, scroll down to the bottom of the page and click the "Other feedback" link.

4. **On the page that appears, compose a note to Facebook's customer service team.** Bear in mind that Facebook has over 500 million members, so don't expect a quick, personalized response.

Useful Facebook-Related Websites

Facebook's Help feature is the last word on how the site works, and its About Page is the official source of press releases and other goings-on (click the About link at the bottom of any Facebook screen to get to it). But sometimes the most useful info is the stuff that's *not* officially sanctioned. Here are a few of the meatiest sites around:

- **The Facebook Blog** (*http://blog.facebook.com*). Actually, this site *is* officially sanctioned, so keep that in mind. It contains updates, tips, and explanations written by people who work for Facebook. This is the place to go when you notice a new feature (or discover that an old one is gone or working differently) and want to know why the site's designers made the change—and what you can expect next.

- **Inside Facebook** (*www.insidefacebook.com*). This independent blog tracks Facebook's evolving business model with a clear, critical eye. It's a good site to check out if you're using Facebook to advertise yourself or your company.

- **All Facebook** (*www.allfacebook.com*). This blog is a good place to read up on controversial Facebook issues and draw your own conclusions. It's great if you want to be in the know about Facebook.

- **Community-powered support for Facebook** (*http://getsatisfaction. com/facebook*). You can find questions (and answers) about unexpected Facebook behavior on this unofficial discussion board. It's a great resource if you've posted something to Facebook's Help discussion board and just can't wait until someone gets back to you.

Index